C/o John McNamara,

Very proud to hear
of your success —

Vern Mills

VERN MILLER: LEGENDARY KANSAS LAWMAN

MIKE DANFORD

IUNIVERSE, INC.
NEW YORK   BLOOMINGTON

Vern Miller: Legendary Kansas Lawman

The views expressed in this work are solely those of the author and do not necessarily reflect the views of the publisher, and the publisher hereby disclaims any responsibility for them.

iUniverse books may be ordered through booksellers or by contacting:

iUniverse
1663 Liberty Drive
Bloomington, IN 47403
www.iuniverse.com
1-800-Authors (1-800-288-4677)

Because of the dynamic nature of the Internet, any Web addresses or links contained in this book may have changed since publication and may no longer be valid.

ISBN: 978-1-4401-7180-2 (sc)
ISBN: 978-1-4401-7182-6 (dj)
ISBN: 978-1-4401-7181-9 (ebk)

Printed in the United States of America

iUniverse rev. date: 9/18/2009

Our thanks to our families and friends for their patience while we struggled to put this bit of history in print. It was over five years in the making and lots of it was difficult, so we hope you find this trip back in history enjoyable, enlightening and constructive, flavored with nostalgia.

CONTENTS

We'd like to express our gratitude to the following for their help in the research of the historical archives needed to compile this story.

Bill Miskell & Frances Breyne, Public Information Officers, Kansas Dept. Of Corrections

Deb Bagby, Wichita Eagle News Librarian

Marsha Stenholm & Michelle Enke, Wichita City Library—Local History Section

Bill Caldwell, Archivist for the Joplin Globe

Brian Moline and Virgil Dean, Kansas Historical Society

Our profound thanks to all of those who contributed to the color and flavor of the stories herein by re-telling them to me from their point of view as they saw the events when they happened.

Charlie Lutkie, Sheriff's Captain and Head Jailer for Vern

Neil Myers, retired Wichita Police Detective

Wally Hanks, Vern's first motorcycle partner and later worked for Vern as a Prosecuting Attorney's Investigator

Ernie McRae, ex-FBI agent, defense attorney

Donny Gasser, Vern's bad penny

Keith Sanborn, ex-Sedgwick County Prosecuting Attorney

Al Rush, retired Chief of the Kansas Highway Patrol

Cliff Eden who worked after hours and Sundays at the Jet Club during the Fifties, saw the graft and was sometimes involved in the payoffs

Woody Woodard, remembers the racial tensions of the 50's, enjoyed the nightlife of "colored town" and saw Vern's heyday as a nightclub bouncer

Syd Werbin was a Sheriff's Detective and also served as an Investigator for Vern when he was Attorney General

A History Lesson

History is the word we use to describe the view of what we see when we turn from where we are today to look back at where we've come from. Bear in mind that world history is a bit like a huge rope that's constantly under construction as time moves forward. From that perspective, we can see that Vern Miller has contributed greatly to the size and strength of the rope that is the history of the great state of Kansas as it is today. As a boy, he aspired to be a warrior and once he attained that, he realized that he was the champion for all of the little guys in our state. Today he's evolved still further into an elder statesman in the field of justice, still a champion for the underdog.

To set the stage for his story I'll begin by glossing briefly over the one hundred years following close on the heels of the Old Wild West, which included huge losses of human life from World Wars I and II. Then there were gross profits for a few from Prohibition, the discovery and development of our western oil fields, the Great Depression and the Dust Bowl. Shortly after World War II ended, that period saw our bloody "police action" in Korea which quickly turned into a full-fledged war with North Korea, which was being funded by the USSR and manned by Red China. This was a huge attempt to win the 40 years of Cold War between the Communist countries and the free world. It was a political/economic conflict that kept the entire world poised on the brink of nuclear holocaust for those decades. Next came the extremely costly war in Viet Nam and now we're currently involved in a struggle for human freedom in the Middle East where democracy is a relative newcomer. Here at home, the cultural impacts of back-to-back illegal alcohol and drug escalations of the Roaring 20s, Beatnik and Flower Child generations (more drugs and alcohol) and most recently, the radical differences between the X and Y generations in the manufacturing sector got us to where we are today.

Generally speaking, by the end of WWI the previously acceptable practice of openly wearing a sidearm and the accompanying six-gun justice had become a thing of the past. However, social frictions in the land of boots,

1

buckles and cowboy hats remained, so personal conflicts were more often settled by contests of the fist and our population was growing rapidly in that period. The general public had a 'hard-work' mentality that still contained a degree of rowdiness. Combative confrontations always have the potential for escalation, so by 1950 there was a rapidly growing need for peace officers in Sedgwick County.

With that brief over-view of history as background, we can focus more tightly on his life and career, the people of Kansas that he protected during his career and his lifelong, dedicated commitment to Justice and the Criminal Justice System.

Early in his young adult life, Vern recognized that the laws that we make are the fabric of our society and he wanted to be part of it. Rules are the outline s of acceptable behavior, so law and order to prevent violence and avoid chaos had become his passion that lives on today. He knew that we needed rules to live by, that somebody had to enforce them and that realization drove him forward in his pursuit of peace and justice. Over the three decades that he served us as a peace officer, stories of his escapades have been re-told so often that he's become a legendary character and legends have a way of getting changed, usually enhanced with each successive re-telling, so we might set some of the stories straight here even if some of the few remaining eyewitnesses disagree. To put this all as simply as possible, there's no need to exaggerate Vern's accomplishments because there were an abundance of witnesses, recordings and photographs. Now what constitutes a legendary character is usually an action that seems to have been above the ability of normal people and his or her action is based primarily on the circumstances that are dangerous, sometimes even deadly. Those actions are usually self-sacrificing performances during or after either natural disasters or man-made conflicts.

Next we have a list of a few of Vern's accomplishments that have catapulted him to legendary lawman status. He was:

The first elected County Marshal in Kansas to initiate pro-active law enforcement by staging drug raids outside his assigned territory as well as inside his jurisdiction.

The only county marshal in Kansas to be elected later to the office of Sheriff.

The only Sheriff in Kansas to become an attorney.

The only Sheriff on record who personally pursued and captured a fugitive in another state.

The only Sheriff in the United States to be elected Attorney General of his state.

He was later elected District Attorney of Sedgwick County.

That's quite a string of exciting accomplishments, but there's still more. He's also the only man in recorded history to:

Stage a legal train robbery. Kansas was a dry state at the time and Vern had received numerous complaints from citizens that liquor was being served on the Amtrak trains. In his capacity as the Attorney General of Kansas, he stopped one of their trains and confiscated all of their booze. His action was later approved and upheld by the United States Supreme Court when Amtrak immediately filed suit to prevent him from raiding more of their trains.

He planned and executed the most and the biggest drug and gambling raids ever in the State of Kansas.

He was the first Kansas peace officer to form a championship Golden Gloves boxing team and he recruited primarily from neighborhoods with lots of boys who were at high risk of dropping out of school, not to mention their inherent risk of getting crossways with the law.

In order to show how and why his character and personality developed as it did, it's necessary to briefly mention some parts of his childhood and hit the highlights from there on until his first job as a policeman. After that, the adventure level of his story increases and it reads like a character who's been glamorized by Hollywood or television, somewhat along the lines of Wyatt Earp, Bat Masterson, the Lone Ranger and Roy Rogers all rolled into one. Now bear in mind that Vern is a very real man who lives and breathes to the letter of the Law, the written "..Will of the People". By the way, he resents being compared to any or all of those characters that have been so shamelessly glamorized by Hollywood.

Character attributes play a large part here, so here are a few of his major characteristics. Vern has a tremendous drive to go forward, refusing to dwell long on history except as a reference or to reminisce briefly about some humorous incident. His attitude is very much an "Ok, we got that problem fixed, so what's next?" He is still bluntly, sometimes painfully honest, a trait not often attributed to people in his line of work. He has no fear of failure or for his own safety and he always has a tremendous sense of being in the right. That explains some of his many acts of what the news media recognizes as courage. Then there's his enjoyment of competition; he loves it. The next higher level of competition is combat and he revels in that too, whether it's boxing or football. Again and again I found scattered throughout the hundreds of news articles the adjectives "scrappy, feisty, fearless, competitive" and "committed" as one journalist after another used them to describe Vern. Those of us who know him shrug and grin, then usually follow that with "Yup, that's Vern alright." Oh yeah, he's not into whining about how the world or Mother Nature treats him, either.

Vern has always been committed to playing by the established rules regardless of whether it was a sport that he enjoyed or the rules of our society. Regarding his attitude toward the laws that we've passed to govern ourselves and our behaviors, it's more than safe to say that he was and is committed to the Law. Now 'commitment' to any profession doesn't simply observe a clock or calendar nor does it stop at an eight hour day or a forty hour week under fluorescent lights. It means eating, sleeping and breathing the job, its goals and all that goes with it, every minute of every day. The time of day that the job required his attention as a peace officer was frequently inconvenient and detrimental to his private life, was often dangerous and as often as not, even the weather was absolutely miserable.

During various parts of his lifetime he's been labeled 'Super Cop', 'The General' and 'Super Sheriff' and of course, some that aren't fit for polite company. It's certainly worthy of note that those nicknames came from folks on both sides of the Law, some of whom had some real serious credentials and others who had some equally serious rap sheets, so regardless which side of the law the names came from, they show the respect for the man. The upshot though, is that this story is about how he did it and much of what he's accomplished, but it's also a serious example for the rest of us by showing us that whatever it is that we want or need to do it can be done if we simply set ourselves to the task and stick to it. Frankly, many of us who know him fully expect that his epitaph will read simply that "He was the ultimate lawman" and his legacy to us will be the very definition of the word 'accomplishment'. He set the example for law enforcement in this state based on conditions at the time and he set the bar extremely high for many generations to follow.

Like most heroes and legendary characters, Vern doesn't crave notoriety or fame. Actually, he'd just as soon be rather low-key. If it weren't for the truckload of historical accountings in the newspaper clippings about Vern, many of these incidents wouldn't even be remembered by now, much less put to print. In the simplest terms, he tried to keep the bad guys alive, black eyes, split lips, busted noses, cracked skulls, broken teeth and all. One of his many quotes that attest to this humane philosophy is that "Weapons should be used not to kill, but to keep the peace" (as deterrents to the escalation of violence, the very last resort).

As lawmen and keepers of the peace, our lawmen have been remarkably effective, but history tells us that peace keeping was just a job to most of the lawmen of the Old West, including the Earps and Mastersons. Then along came Vern. He was and is a type A personality, aggressive and competitive, even fiercely combative when the situations required it. He rose through the ranks of law enforcement from Deputy Sheriff on a motorcycle to County Marshal, then Sheriff, on to Attorney General of the State of Kansas and finally as Prosecuting Attorney of Sedgwick County. Last but certainly not least, today he's reached what he considers the pinnacle of his career; he's a criminal defense attorney in private practice. "I don't want to help a criminal to continue being a criminal, I want to help people solve their behavior problems and live like good citizens." Notice that the word "help" is prominent in his philosophy. He's been that way from the first day he donned a badge and began untangling traffic snarls, sometimes changing tires for stranded motorists and in extreme circumstances to defending those who couldn't defend themselves, sometimes even against the legal system itself. He's always been a peace officer in one form or another.

Vern is very well-educated and articulate. He's a bundle of energy in constant, contagious motion and athletically he's always been well above average, but in his fifty year career in law enforcement has only fired his gun at another human being on one occasion. Well, maybe two, but he only hit one of those and even he claims that it was blue ribbon luck that he even got close to hitting a moving target at 40 yards with a short-barreled pistol while both he and his target were running wide open.

Now Vern views our Law as being the only defense of civilized Man against the Primitive. In addition, Vern sees the Law as an opportunity to accomplish something everyday while helping to keep us all moving forward pointed in the right direction. He knows that for peace to reign requires levelheaded reason, the Law of the People.... and to Vern those laws are sacred. They are the rules we've written to meet the needs of the people so that we can all go about our lives without fear and in peace.

If we learn any lessons from studying human history, one of them is that men and women who perform extraordinary feats under extreme duress are frequently labeled heroes and are accorded all the honors that go with the title, such as parades, naming streets and schools after them. Over time their stories become legends with the exaggeration and spin of the re-tellings, especially since they're likely to repeat their acts of heroism periodically as the need arises. This story is all about just such a man and, believe it or not, he's a humble realist. He's a living, legendary hero who used his remarkable strength, his lack of fear, his seemingly boundless energy and his huge love of the laws of our society to make a better place for the rest of us to live. His basic premise is almost a moral in itself; "If you don't agree with a law, change it, but don't break it."

Since no other opportunity to mention his family presents itself in the story, I'll tell you here that Vern has three sons and a daughter, all grown now and he's very proud of them. Both Marty and Cliff have been police officers, Chris is an adopted son who works in construction and Jamie Rose works for Roto Rooter. It's a tightly bonded group and yes, it's had its share of problems and heartaches as well as astounding accomplishments, but their affection for each other is truly amazing to observe.

What makes it so difficult for us to recognize real, live heroes is that they're right in among us, living right next door, breathing, loving, working, carrying out the trash, making their fair share of mistakes and doing all the small, daily chores that make us all human. They look like us and usually behave very much like the rest of us until some certain set of circumstances sets off their exceptional behavior. At the time of this writing, at least one of our very real-life heroes is still with us. Vern's still practicing law, occasionally riding one of his motorcycles, going to church, being a grandfather and playing like all the rest of us. As he always has, he's enjoying his allotted time here.

SOMETIME IN 2003

It was a blistering hot Kansas afternoon outside as I sat watching Vern from the couch in his modest, unpretentious office where the atmosphere was comfortably cool. This was his first look at how the story was progressing, so he was understandably critical and his input was exactly what I needed to get the whole story. He sat across the room at his desk while he read my first draft on the screen of my laptop computer. Generally speaking, there are two types of biographies; one is a documentary type that is rather dry because it doesn't include the "feel good" information such as weather conditions regardless how beautiful or severe, emotions of the characters, facial expressions, observations of witnesses and onlookers, etceteras. We realized right up front that a dry documentary wasn't the type of story we wanted to write, so I made quick notes when he shook his head and commented periodically that I'd made a mistake on a detail or a date here and there. It was great fun to watch him grin and chuckle occasionally as he was a reminded of an incident that he hadn't thought of for a long time and I knew that he'd tell me the story as he'd seen it unfold. Some of the history he was reading dated back well over fifty years, so it was understandable why he'd sometimes stumble remembering some of the names, but he knew that we had the newspaper clippings to back up each individual story and he remembers the details of most of those cases very clearly.

Many of us have concluded that people generally fall into three categories, those being 'thinkers, talkers and do-ers'. Vern's an exceptionally good combination of all three and because he's a thinker, he's sensitive to the embarrassment and pain that a 'misbehaver' can cause friends and family just as well as the warm feeling of pride in a friend or relative who achieves an admirable goal. Because of this, we've chosen to leave out a few of the names in some of the stories rather than hurt some of the people involved and their families by reminding them of ancient embarrassments. Then there's the "talker" side of him; he's very articulate and extremely capable of cramming a lot of words into very little time. Last but certainly not least, he's action-prone. The phrase "Git 'er done" used by the U.S. Army could've been coined because of him because he's never been one to sit on his hands.

Doing the research for this story has been a real trip. The easy part was tracking down a quite a few old-timers who are still alive to get their slant on something that happened four or five decades ago. It was nice talking to them and they were extremely informative, but the hardest and most productive parts of the research was in the news articles that were written twenty to fifty years ago. Vern's sweet little mother, bless her Protestant heart, had kept many newspaper and magazine clippings about his accomplishments and escapades, so she'd collected several refrigerator-sized cardboard boxes of them over his long career. It's as though she had some knowledge beforehand that her little boy would amount to someone that we'd all admire and eventually write a book about. She was extremely proud of her children and rightfully so, but it was easy to see where she'd run out of the energy to continue building the numerous albums of photographs and huge collection of news articles when she began to simply cut them out of newspapers and toss them into those huge cardboard boxes. At first, I tried to sort those thousands of articles chronologically in order to get a sense of what'd happened in each decade of his life, but there are so many that we wound up just selecting what looked like the most interesting cases. I must warn you that a few of those news photos are brutally graphic records of human pain and sudden death, so if you're sensitive to the sight of human blood, please brace yourself. After I'd assembled the outstanding articles and photos into a readable form, we found that we'd made a much better-than-average biographical book that we're proud of and we hope you enjoy reading it. This's how it all shook out.

Growing Up, In His Own Words

"My family was definitely among the working class. My father built a big two-story frame house on ten acres that just happened to be close to two of the poorest sections of Wichita; it was located right between Bogtown and Hoover's Orchard. The house was on the southwest corner of Harry and West street which was one corner of our acreage, way out in the country back then; it kept us warm, dry and happy for many years. The whole family loved that old house and my folks lived in it until Dad died in 1954. That was my first serious experience with emotional pain and it's one that I'll never forget. Not long after Dad died, Mom sold the old homestead and moved into town to live right next door to her church."

Here's a photo of a very young Vern standing on his burro's back on their little farm. Tony (the burro) was always very patient with his young friend and they spent lots of time together in Vern's childhood.

He leaned back in his chair and closed his eyes as he described the times back then. "The streets in our neighborhood weren't paved back then and of course there were no streetlights. The houses of most of our neighbors were ...well,let's just say that they were all small compared to ours. Most of those houses were already quite old, so they needed lots of repairs and TLC, but that cost money. Very few of our neighbors had much more than grocery money, so anything left over after buying food went for rent and if there was any left over it bought a few incidentals, like clothes. Yes, it was indeed a tough neighborhood to grow up in. Us kids often fought for fun and bragging rights in our neighborhood. We played a lot of rough sandlot football without pads or helmets and many of the kids from around there belonged to a real tough bunch called the Hoover's Orchard Gang. Although I didn't belong to that one or any other gang, I considered it an honor that they frequently reached outside their own ranks to ask me to represent them in the Friday night bare-knuckle fistfights under the bridge at Douglas and McClean Boulevard. There wasn't any malice in it and since it was just good, clean fun, the cops left us alone to put knots on each others' heads and chip each other's teeth. Sometimes when business was slow for them, the cops even joined the crowds to watch and cheer on their favorites. Since nobody had much money, bets were very small and nearly always one-on-one. Oh yeah, we were sticklers for playing by the established rules, so kicking, knees and weapons were outlawed and I can't remember about biting in the clinches, but I'm sure it wasn't allowed either. Those were bare-knuckle fistfights and a cheater could sustain more than damage to just his reputation if he broke the rules and the crowd didn't like it. Simply put, honor was paramount. "

Here's some more of his colorful personal history. Vern was valedictorian of his eighth-grade class at Eureka Grade School and he thinks it's funny to mention that there'd only been thirty to forty of his classmates vying for the title. Then he went on through Allison Intermediate and graduated from Wichita High School North. He was a fairly good student all the way through school and he developed into a very good, three-sport athlete in high school, lettering in football, basketball and track. Below are pictures of the North High School basketball, football teams and one for the track team where he really excelled as a runner and a member of the State Champion mile relay team in 1946. The old bicycle that he'd ridden five miles each way to his first year of high school had played a large part in his physical development, but he traded it off in his junior year. He traded that bicycle for an old motorcycle and walked right into a love affair with motorcycles that he still enjoys today, more than sixty years later.

This is one version of the North High track team that ultimately won the State Champion mile relay in 1946.

The next photo is of the basketball team; that's 'Mule' Miller's bright and shiny face on the front row, closest to the camera. By the way, there are two popular theories about how he got that nickname. One is that getting hit by either of his fists was like getting kicked by a mule and the other was directly attributable to his dogged tenacity on the football field. Knowing him, I'd say it could be either or both, but he claims that his football coach, A.B. Collum gets credit for it. Anyway, in the picture it's easy to tell by his big, boyish grin that he was really enjoying the moment, as always. Of course he didn't know it back then, but he was heading toward getting involved in the affairs of the world far beyond his school years as a fearless leader and a remarkable pace setter.

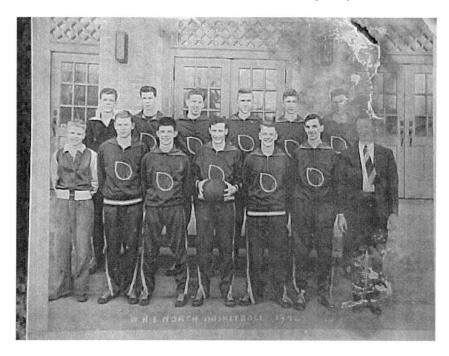

Here's the photo of the football team and once again he's on the front row, this time second from right.

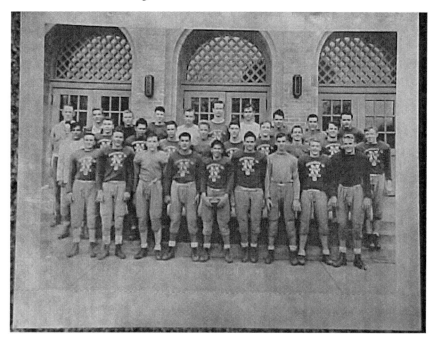

A Young Soldier,
Homesick In Korea

It was a feisty, extremely energetic teenager that enlisted in the U.S. Army right out of high school and from that point his energies were well-directed toward a constructive end. The Army took over his life, polished his self-discipline, honed his focus and satisfied his need for physical combat with huge amounts of constant exercise to consume all of that energy and sent him to Korea immediately after boot camp. The political/social climate there was extremely unstable in that region in the aftermath of the devastation of World War II. Completely unaware that the stage was being set for the invasion from North Korea, the free world was pouring money and technology into post-war Japan as well as South Korea in an attempt to rebuild the devastated regional economy. U.S. troops were in Korea as part of a United Nations police action to round up a few Japanese soldiers isolated in the mountains; they didn't know that the war was over and a few Communist agitators who were aware of it simply made trouble. Vern spent his eighteenth birthday in Korea and as he puts it, he "...Was one real homesick kid".

Here's Vern in battle gear in Korea, 1947

There are no photographs or newspaper articles to draw from, but from Vern's memory comes the revelation that the Army is where his professional boxing career almost started. It's where he learned to do it right and fairly well, so he enjoyed it. No, he doesn't remember his win-loss record, but with tongue in cheek he says he probably won as many as he lost. However, within a few short months of his arrival in Korea his health began to fail and it was quickly discovered that he'd contracted rheumatic fever, so he was sent home where he received treatment, then a medical discharge before the North Koreans suddenly crossed the 38th parallel. Mother Nature had ended his chances of ever acquiring a professional license to box for money and moved him out of the way of a real serious shooting war.

However, he was back at home where he really wanted to be and his only scar was a heart murmur that would haunt him for the rest of his life. Only his family and a few close friends were aware it and although it didn't slow him down athletically, he's always known that it was there.

Although his time in the Army had been cut short by Mother Nature, the gregarious kid from Kansas has some favorite memories of his time in Korea.

Here's a photo of a group of orphans that he and his buddies befriended. Like so many other GI's far from home and on foreign soil, he and his buddies quickly developed a big brother relationship with some of the orphaned children and quietly did as much as they could for their little Korean friends. Vern's in the center of the photo without a cap.

THE MOTORCYCLE COP

1948: This picture was taken on his first day of work as a Deputy Sheriff. Notice the lack of a motorcycle helmet? They came into use several years later. The picture was taken at his parent's farm. He's wearing his new uniform with a borrowed Colt 38 that had a long, six-inch barrel and he's leaning on one of the four brand new 1948 Harley Davidson Electraglides owned by the Sheriff's department.

Here's how he got into his new line of work. Like most soldiers just home from service in a foreign land, he got married shortly after he got back into civilian clothes and with another mouth to feed, he was immediately looking for work. One day he saw an ad in the paper for motorcycle riders to apply to the Sheriff's department, so off he went to the County Courthouse. Sure enough, Captain Jack Tucker, who was Sheriff Bob Grey's road patrol captain was standing outside on the steps, smoking a cigarette. They talked briefly and, of course, Captain Tucker asked if he could ride a cycle. To prove that he knew how to handle a motorcycle, Vern climbed on one of the shiny new Harleys and rode it around the block to prove his skill and Jack hired him on the spot without a physical exam or background check. His burning desire to be a gladiator had been rekindled and he was thrilled! Vern was told to go to Brick's Men's Clothing Store to buy a uniform, the department issued him a badge, he borrowed a gun, then he went to work that very same evening to help straighten out the shift-change messes being made three times each day by the Boeing traffic.

Wichita Beacon Jan. 27, 1967

He was in heaven. Making traffic move smoothly was apparently something he'd always wanted to try and he quickly discovered that he was very good at it. We had to use a much later photo to make the point, but you can see that he really knew what he was doing.

Those of us who are old enough to remember our narrow streets, highways and lack of traffic control lights shudder at the thought of commuter traffic back then and some of us even remember seeing him in action on the streets and highways in and around Wichita. Vern was a quick-study, so he became very good at untying the snarls, keeping the traffic of the tired aircraft workers flowing smoothly and he really enjoyed riding the big, noisy Harleys of the early Fifties, especially with his first partner, veteran traffic officer Wally Hanks.

One day shortly after he signed on for this job the weather turned a little nasty, so Vern and Wally drove a police car rather than ride the Harleys to their traffic assignment. As they arrived at George Washington Boulevard and Oliver they found traffic stacked up for a mile on each side of the intersection and just as they got out of the car to untangle the snarl, a huge guy on a motorcycle came riding between the lanes of traffic, which is illegal in Kansas. Wally flagged the guy down and told him he'd get a ticket if he didn't stop it. The guy argued, so Wally disgustedly turned to shut off the traffic control light and told Vern to write the ticket. Wouldn't you know it, just as Vern started writing the ticket, the guy gunned his engine and dropped the clutch to ride away. Vern dropped the ticket book and jumped on the biker's back, bringing the bike and rider down in the middle of the intersection like a bulldogging cowboy! It was a great wrestling/punching match for a few seconds until Wally arrived with the handcuffs. It took awhile to wear the guy down, but between the two of them they finally got their belligerent customer into the back seat of their police car where he had to wait until they got the traffic flowing again and then they all went down to the jailhouse. Yes, traffic was **really** backed up by that time!

The two scrappy cops were pleased to have been so well-matched and their careers crossed paths many times over the next several decades. In later years when Vern was the County's Prosecuting Attorney, Wally worked for him as an Investigator so you'll hear more about Wally later.

Wichita Eagle   June 20, 1951

This newspaper article is of significant historical value because it's the first time Vern's name appeared in the news media for action connected to law enforcement.

Vern has never been one to sit on his laurels and even back then he was very perceptive, so it was predictable that he'd recognize that the road to upward mobility and success required a college education. He'd enrolled at Friends University for a long succession of courses during the day while he worked as a motorcycle cop at night. It sounds innocent enough so far, but while attending classes he met Howard Mullenix, a mischievous classmate who'd recently lost a license plate to a thief. Well, they quickly became good friends and Howard heckled Vern all semester long about the police not being able to find that purloined tag. Vern could only grin and bear it, giving back the good-natured repartee as best he could, but he memorized that license plate number. SG52904 is burned indelibly into his memory today, over 50 years later.

Then Circumstance stepped in and the unbelievable happened. Several months later as he was on his motorcycle headed for the Boeing complex to work the rush hour traffic, he saw the tag; it was attached to a new Lincoln at approximately South Broadway and Pawnee. On came the red lights and siren in an attempt to get the driver to pull over, but the driver didn't have a peaceful surrender in mind, so the chase was on. They were headed south on Broadway across the John Mack Bridge, weaving through the traffic of startled citizens and sometimes exceeding speeds well above 80 mph! A traffic snarl at Broadway and MacArthur finally stopped the Lincoln just long enough for the young officer to slide to a stop, drop his bike and run to the driver's window to tranquilize him with a quick punch, then drag him out through the open window and slap the handcuffs on him. Vern admits sheepishly that he wasn't polite or gentle, but considering the circumstances, it's easy to understand his rough treatment of a driver who'd jeopardized so many innocent lives.

Naturally, the driver later complained loudly about police brutality, but he didn't get much sympathy from a Kansas judge, especially when it was revealed that the car had been stolen in New Mexico in addition to wearing the stolen Kansas license plate. The youthful driver was then turned over to New Mexico authorities for his string of bad judgements, which included crossing state lines with a stolen car.

Vern recognized the opportunity for a little devilment, so he took the tag off the stolen car and presented it to Howard during an extemporaneous speech that was required for the class they were taking together. During that speech he claimed that he'd suspected that the tag had been in Mullinex's garage all along, so he'd got a search warrant to find it. The class roared and Howard was embarrassed, not yet realizing that he was the victim of a practical joke. However, the truth came out the next day when the newspaper told the real story and Howard found himself vindicated.

During the 1950's, Wichita and the surrounding county was experiencing an economic boom which was the direct result of World War II and the following police action in Korea plus the parallel Cold War with the Communist bloc. The Cold War with the USSR evolved into a spending race on weapons delivery systems, so Boeing was roaring wide open on cost-plus programs to build warplanes in huge numbers, which meant that lots of people had much better-paying jobs than they'd ever had and it bloated the local economy. Anybody that would report to work had a job and most of those jobs paid lots better than the labor force had ever earned before. In addition, many families had two incomes for the first time, so many of those couples amassed sizeable savings. Those same wage earners were also spending their new-found wealth and the multiplying effect on the local economy was immense.

Now down through the ages, some people have always worked to be constructive and productive while others, specifically many people in the 'entertainment' industry, try to find out what those workers want to do in their leisure time so they can provide it. That's just simple marketing whether it's for merchandise or services, however, we know that the temptation of easy money, especially if there doesn't appear to be a victim can easily be too much for many. Even some politicians and lawmen have succumbed to the temptation of profiting from that temptation down through the ages. As they had done since the years of Prohibition, some clubs around Wichita and out in the county gladly provided gambling (including slot machines), liquor after hours (Sundays too), prostitutes, a little pot or something more dangerous. It was all available for a price while a percentage of the profit bought the privilege of doing business.

During those years it was said facetiously that a "good" Sheriff should never have to work again after serving a term or two. I was there, I saw some of it and I knew some old-timers who were involved in the clubs that were allowed to operate on Sundays and deep into the nights after the legal closing time and the bootlegging that went on around those neighborhoods. When our young motorcycle officer asked why this was allowed, Vern was told by his superior officers to take care of his Traffic Department and that the problem was being "taken care of" by other departments. He didn't like being told to butt out, but it was obvious that he could do nothing about it ...yet.

About that time a crusading Attorney General named Harold Fatzer attempted to shut down gambling in the state. He sent a team of KBI Officers and Deputy Attorneys General to Wichita specifically to clamp down on slot machines. It appears to have been an deliberate move that Vern was assigned to escort the visiting officers around to places of business that had the machines and the first such place they visited was a skating rink on South Broadway that a man named Jim operated. Jim was obviously expecting them, so he greeted them cheerfully and asked "What's up?" Vern and the other officers kept walking, continuing on their way up the stairs to the second mezzanine. Vern explained the mission to Jim while the small group headed for the spots where Vern had seen the machines just days earlier.

The machines were gone even though the dust on the floor clearly showed the footprints of those missing machines. Jim just shrugged, grinned and feigned innocence. The team was irritated and disappointed, so they left to make other stops. They encountered the same situation wherever they went that night, revealing that there was a serious security leak somewhere, so the Attorney General's Investigators finally gave up and went back to Topeka empty-handed and frustrated. It had not been a good day for the Law in our state. The young officer quietly made a mental note to himself that this fight wasn't over yet.

Like most young policemen down through the ages, Vern's family was growing so he made extra money in his off-duty time by providing security at the local night clubs. He was working as bouncer at the Old Barn Club at MacArthur and Broadway a few nights each week and coincidentally, there was a Teamsters strike in full swing, which meant that a "membership recruiting" team was in town. That's labor union code for the 'muscle' of a strong-arm tactics squad. Among the professional drivers being pressured to join were the taxi drivers of Sedgwick County and quite a few of them had been leaned on pretty hard. One night when Vern was working at his part-time job, a bartender named Dick yelled to Vern that there was a fight in the men's room. Vern reacted quickly. He charged in, saw a taxi driver being held up against a wall and slapped around hard by a burley character, so he grabbed the assailant, hoisted the big guy over his shoulder and carried him outside, kicking and flailing. The fight really started when he dumped the guy on the ground and he came up by grabbing Vern's John Brown gun strap, pulling Vern forward toward him. Vern was much lighter and faster, so rather than give the big guy any advantage he leaned into that first punch real hard, aiming for dead center of his face and the assailant went down on his back. He didn't stay down, though. He kept getting up again and again, but Vern had now had the clear advantage of standing over him, so getting vertical was impossible for the thug. He continued to try it and it got him hit again and again identical to the first punch, each one putting him flat on his back. Then three guys jumped out of a black Cadillac sedan yelling to Vern that they'd take care of him, so Vern backed off and allowed them to carry the groggy, battered and bleeding thug away while Vern went back inside to check on the taxi driver...and soak his bleeding knuckles in cold water.

Within the next hour, Vern recalls that a lot of taxi drivers stopped at the club to thank him for taking care of them and some of those drivers identified the guy Vern had clobbered as Blacky Ferris, a tough-talking Teamster "recruiter" from Chicago. Then came a phone call for Vern; a voice with a Chicago accent challenged him to show up at the T Bone Club on South 47th Street in an hour. Vern knew better than to go alone, so he enlisted the aid of two of the biggest, toughest officers he knew, Bob Harkleroad and Dale Menefee. The "A Team" drove to the T Bone in uniform and waited around for over an hour, glaringly obvious in their uniforms. But there was no sign of the muscle from Chicago. It seems they'd already had enough of the vicious farm boys of Kansas.

Bouncing rowdies and drunks in a nightclub that catered to black Americans back in those days was risky at best, but it was especially dangerous for a white cop even if he was super tough and much-liked by the general patronage. There was such a very popular club in the black section of north Wichita known as Flagler's Garden. It was on east 29th Street North and regularly featured some very popular black musicians and performers, so the crowds were frequently large. A short, stocky, very strong black man named R.D. Hancock ran the popular night spot, but the heavy drinking and frequent fights in and around his club were increasing and that worried him, so he asked the Sheriff for a deputy to work with him to maintain the peace. Sheriff Ty Lockett had just the man in mind for the job, so he sent Vern, who had a reputation for being scrappy when necessary, but always preferring to talk a fight down. Now Vern's reputation for scrapping and brawling had already preceded him, so with just a little advance 'word-of-mouth' advertising by Hancock of Vern's new off-duty assignment, Vern began the new extra-pay job on Friday and Saturday nights as an added attraction, although he was blissfully unaware of that angle.

As expected, there was quite a string of characters who thought they could beat the public's champion, but that didn't happen and they each paid the price for the honor of having met the best. Our guy retained his unofficial title and growing reputation as one of the toughest guys in town and the action settled down considerably around Hancock's nightclub. One of the most decisive nights was one particular Saturday night. Vern was fighting with a rowdy customer who was pretty good at brawling when the man suddenly sagged to the floor, then went completely limp. He was out like a light. Vern was alarmed and yelled "R.D., he must be having a heart attack! I sure didn't hit him hard enough to do that."

R.D. wasn't at all concerned; he just grinned and replied calmly, "Aw, don't worry about it, Vern. Just feel that knot behind his right ear."

Vern says sheepishly that he'd begun to think that he was the world's all-time knockout king when R.D. revealed that he'd been sapping most of Vern's opponents with a blackjack, so many of Vern's opponents had a knot the size of an egg behind one of their ears. Well, Vern was disappointed to find that he didn't have some kind of magic knockout punch, but he met some real nice people on that job. As a matter of fact, many of the rowdies that he swapped a few punches with at Flagler's became loyal friends and it got downright peaceful around there after awhile, which of course made R.D real happy.

The comments of an interview with a very respectable, elderly black gentleman who'd witnessed lots of Vern's fights are interesting. The portly old gentleman leaned back in his rocking chair in the shade of his front porch with his hands folded across his generous midriff as he delved back into his memories of many decades earlier. He barely noticed the arrival of a tall glass of iced tea that a granddaughter set carefully on the end table next to his chair before politely delivering mine with a gentle smile. For a while, he recalled the good times, the happiness of those much younger years and then the brawls, finally getting to those that involved the toughest guy in town at that time, Vern Miller. "Y'know", the old man reminisced, "Watching Vern do what he did so well was a lot like watching an over-sized Jack Russell terrier on steroids. He was so fast that most guys didn't see his fists coming and even those that saw them couldn't get out of the way most of the time. For us boxing fans, it was fascinating to watch his hand-speed and the power he could put into any one of those punches was amazing!' Why, I saw him lift one 230 lb guy off his feet by his front teeth!"…and he chuckled. "Vern spotted most of them guys forty to fifty pounds, sometimes lots more, and still showed them how it was done!" Eventually, the old man nodded off and I left quietly, smiling goodbye to the granddaughter as I tiptoed off the porch.

One of the many folks he met at Flagler's was Olivia McNairy, a stocky, muscular black woman with a history of mental/emotional problems who worked as a "boner" for Cudahy Meat Packing. She was nice enough, maybe even downright pleasant when she was sober and level, but a real bad customer when boozed up. Vern had encountered her several times in the club when she'd misbehaved and she'd put some dandy cuts on his arms with a knife. During the encounter when she cut him, he'd even drawn his pistol but he put it away when she showed that she wasn't the least bit intimidated. At that point, the fight was a draw with a standoff. Ultimately, he refused to shoot her when he realized that she didn't or couldn't understand the finality of the danger she faced. His decision to put the pistol back in it's holster cost him some more blood and a lot of stitches before he finally managed to subdue her.

Wichita Eagle May 25, 1954

They met again one last time in May of 1954. Mrs. McNairy had been released from the Kansas State Mental Hospital at Larned several weeks earlier when the call came over Vern's radio to respond to a domestic disturbance at an address well known to law officers because of numerous domestic violence calls there. Vern and Deputy Dale Menefee responded, but they were still several blocks from the address when they saw Mrs. McNairy staggering along the street covered with blood. She was dazed and offered no resistance whatever as they took her into custody. They arrived at her home to find her common-law husband dead of stab wounds, so the coroner was called. Mrs. McNairy had stabbed Theodore Daniels, aka Pete Overstreet to death.

She was arraigned quickly and during the proceeding, she begged the presiding judge, George Ashford to allow her to see her beloved one last time. In a rare deviation from procedure, Judge Ashford ordered Vern to accompany her across the street to the mortuary, so across the street they went, handcuffed together. Vern had made a serious mistake by handcuffing his right arm to her left arm. Upon viewing her loved one in the coffin, Olivia immediately became emotionally overwrought, wrapped her right arm around her dead husband's head, pulling him to her for a last embrace. Hoping to reduce her emotional distress, Vern attempted to pull Olivia away, but she lifted the corpse right out of the coffin and all three fell to the floor. Vern found himself at the bottom of a three-body pile until some of the funeral home employees arrived to sort them out.

It took a while and considerable assistance from the funeral home workers, but the lady eventually calmed down and was returned to a cell, whereupon Vern went straight to the judge and after telling his story, he requested that in the future that similar humanitarian requests be considered more carefully. The judge roared with laughter and after he regained his composure, he agreed not to grant any more humanitarian requests of that sort.

Then there's the story of one New Year's Eve party at a Latino club at 25th and North Broadway where his notoriety worked against him. Vern had been hired to keep the peace, but a boisterous couple created an incident at the front door. After ejecting the couple, who'd been drinking heavily, a scuffle with some troublesome bystanders ensued. Several uniformed soldiers in the crowd didn't like the odds against Vern, so they came to his assistance. The tide had turned and the fight was over in a hurry. Vern went back inside, dusting himself off and straightening up his uniform. He was still running on adrenaline, so he told the guys that'd agitated those scuffles that they'd better shape up and the situation began to heat up again. Finally, the club operator intervened; he pulled Vern aside to say quietly "Vern, how much do I owe you for your time so far? Here! I'll pay you for the whole shift. You're causing more trouble than you're solving, so go home! I don't need you any longer." It's funny to watch him tell that story with a sheepish grin and his characteristic chuckle.

Wichita Eagle July 12, 1951

Vern and his captain, Floyd Schroeder were doing flood-rescue duty near Marion, Kansas when their boat overturned, dumping all the occupants into the raging waters. Schroeder couldn't swim, but Vern was an excellent swimmer, so Vern got Floyd and the flood victims to the safety of a stranded cattle truck whose stock racks were still well above water. Suddenly, Vern got swept away by the strong current. He was carried well over half a mile downstream before he could make it to shore and he was exhausted, so it was a long, slow walk back to the rescue site. Meantime, the rescue crew had arrived, tight-roped them all to safety and heard the sad news about his apparent drowning. Assuming the worst, they notified their dispatcher who relayed the news back to Wichita and someone in the Sheriff's office made the rash decision to notify Vern's mother before the news was confirmed. Naturally, when Vern suddenly reappeared, a cheer went up and there was a great rush to correct the news. Now the connection between this incident and the one just below is that Vern and Floyd had both changed into bathing suits, then they'd folded their uniforms and put them into the boat that had overturned and sunk, so both uniforms were lost.

Wichita Eagle July 16, 1951

Uniform #2 went to uniform heaven as most uni's do sooner or later; it was rendered unfit for duty in a brawl, as most of them are. The article title reads "Deputy Sheriff Hit On Head By Tube of Rubber Cement" and as alway there's lots more to the story, but the reporter didn't manage to get all of this story into print. Vern was sent to an injury-auto accident and found Mr. & Mrs. John Wilson were slightly injured and very inebriated. Vern says "Hey, they weren't just inebriated; they were staggering drunk!" The story they gave Vern was that they'd been thrown out of a car driven by friends they'd been riding with who eventually abandoned them alongside a busy highway. The article is vague when it fails to mention why Vern had decided to take the pair to jail, but it was probably for public drunk and disorderly. Mr. Wilson objected to being taken into custody, so a scuffle ensued and, of course, Mrs. Wilson decided to join the fray. She found a tube of rubber cement in the back seat of the patrol car and chose to use it as a weapon. She pounded Vern on the head with it until the tube split, spilling its gooey, sticky contents all over his head, his face, his uniform, then it got smeared all over the upholstery of his police car after he subdued the couple and drove the two miscreants to jail. He spent over two hours using turpentine to get the messy upholstery cleaned up and of course, the uniform was ruined. All that turpentine wasn't good for his complexion, either; he looked pretty raw for several days afterward and he took a lot of ribbing, heckling and teasing about his appearance.

By 1954, Ty Lockett had served the limit of four years as Sheriff and three of his deputies chose to run for the office. They were Walter Koob (the Under-Sheriff), Jim Underwood (the Chief Investigator) and Floyd Schroeder (Captain of the road patrol). Sheriff Lockett required them all to resign while they campaigned for office, which resulted in Vern's promotion to Captain of the road patrol (traffic control).

The Sheriff's office was elective and it was nearly impossible for the uniformed officers not to take sides at election time, so the situation had become highly political even for the non-elective deputies. Well, it's a given that strong personalities often clash and sometimes even erupt in physical conflict, especially if they've been friends since childhood. It was a disagreement over political tactics that caused Vern and his old friend Floyd Schroeder to clash and when Vern tried to smooth the friction between them, the conversation quickly took a wrong turn and escalated, punches were thrown and it turned into a donnybrook that only ended when Schroeder suffered a broken nose, ending the fight. Vern drove Floyd to the old Wichita Hospital at Seneca and Douglas for treatment, but that wasn't the end of it. Vern then switched his support from Schroeder to Underwood, Floyd won the election and Vern had backed the wrong candidate for Sheriff, so he was out of a job on Jan 11, 1955.

HIS GAS STATION

What looked like a great opportunity to operate his own business came along in the form of an eight-pump gas station down on South Broadway which was U.S. 81, the major north-south highway through Wichita at the time. Vern turned in his badge and motorcycle, put away his gun and bought the station. He took his seemingly boundless energy and enthusiasm, his recently acquired degree in Business Administration and went to work pumping gas, changing sparkplugs and washing windshields. Sure enough, the money began rolling in and life was good. At just about the same time, he got involved in the Democratic Party's activities at the local level with whatever small chunks of his time he could spare from his business. He'd never made as much money in his life as he did from that gas station, but he had a burning desire to be a law officer that far outweighed the lure of money, so when the Party needed a candidate for the position of County Marshal, young Vern tossed his hat in the ring.

As frequently happens around salvage yards, like G & R Salvage which was right next door to Vern's gas station, there were usually a few rowdy-cowboy-teenaged boys hanging around drinking pop and soaking up the atmosphere. On normal days, some of them were in the shop tricking up an engine and a few more were usually lounging around the office guarding the pop machine. About the most exciting daily events in Fred Gray's place of business were the arrival of a wrecked car hauled in on the back of a truck or a rousing game of keep-away football with the resident junkyard Doberman.

This particular day suddenly became unusual because Vern was obviously excited when he ran in from his gas station next door asking for help. He'd just decided to run for County Marshal and he needed someone to watch his cash register while he went to the County courthouse to file for the office. Ironically, one of those rowdy-cowboy, hotrod-building teenagers that volunteered to help was the guy that's writing this story today, so you'll understand when I try to sneak one past Vern (a.k.a. Ol' Straight Arrow). Well, several of us volunteered to help him out, so he took off for downtown and I ambled across the parking lot to pump gas for him for a few hours. That little stint at volunteering turned into several months of standing in for him while he campaigned. He'd played a lotta football, enough to know that forward motion is the only way to make progress, so he talked to everyone who looked old enough to vote, got a few of them registered and naturally, he urged us kids to solicit our parent's votes for him. Darned if he didn't get elected, so he had to hire someone full time to run the gas station and I had to go back to high school.

Wichita Eagle Nov., 1957

He'd won handily, so he had a few weeks to get his private business in order before assuming the duties of the office. Toward that end, he was sitting at his desk in the gas station doing the usual paperwork when frantic car horns and the screech of numerous sets of tires on the four lane highway (U.S. 81) right in front of his gas station got his attention. He looked out the window and saw a 250 pound pig wandering around on the four-lane highway completely disrupting traffic, so Vern dashed out to herd the hapless pig out of the traffic and over into the driveway of his gas station. As luck would have it, Sheriff-elect Denver Bland was a Sheriff's Captain at the time and he just happened to be driving by, arriving just in time to help. A guy named "Cactus Jack" Rylant and his brother "Boogy" showed up and the four of them managed to corral the pig in the grease rack room of the gas station. Back in those days there was no such thing as a County dog catcher much less and official pig catcher, so after they'd all got their second wind, they wrestled the hog into the back seat of Bland's patrol car. Ownership of the pig had been established by phone, so with Vern sitting on top of the squealing, squirming, protesting porker, they returned the rambling hog to its home at Harvey Farney's pig farm about a mile south of Vern's gas station. Harvey was very grateful for the return of his pig and it's reasonable to assume that the pig was happy to be back where food was plentiful and life was considerably more peaceful.

Future Officials Perform 'Hog' Duty

Two county officials-elect, Vern Miller and Denver Bland, found serving the public a real chore Wednesday. Bland is captain of the sheriff's patrol and Miller formerly headed the patrol.

A hog strayed from its owner's farm at 5000 S. Broadway and onto U.S. Highway 81, causing a traffic problem.

Miller, marshal-elect of Commission Pleas Court, saw the 250-pound animal from the window of his service station at 4125 S. Broadway.

He summoned his assistant and a nearby garageman and the trio lassoed the hog and pulled and prodded it into a big ice box near the station.

The hog began tearing up the ice box so Miller and his assistant removed it to the grease room of the station.

He called the sheriff's office and asked that the animal be picked up.

Sheriff-elect Bland, unaware that the offender was a hog, appeared at the service station in a patrol car.

The hog was wrestled into the back seat of the car and with Miller sitting on top of it, re-

Just two days before Vern was to win the election, he and Bill Warfield had just closed the gas station for the night and drove north on Broadway in Bill's new Chevy that sported a "Miller for Marshal" poster on each side. Another car pulled alongside them wanting to race at each stoplight and there were some uncomplimentary words exchanged after each race and the rhetoric became increasingly heated. Finally, Bill had enough and pulled into a parking lot at Harry and Broadway, thinking the other car would simply drive away. Nope, it didn't happen that way. Instead, the driver pulled in close behind them and the passenger got out, obviously looking for trouble. Vern was out of the car first, just as the big guy charged, bellowing something to the effect that somebody was going to get something whipped as he charged with his arms spread wide, one of the classic (although not good) attack-stances. It was a one-punch fight. Outweighed by way over fifty pounds, our lightning-fast welterweight moved left to avoid the lunge, then put everything he had into that first punch and the blockbuster landed right on the big guy's nose, splattering it like a ripe tomato. The big guy was staggered and his knees buckled, but he didn't go all the way down. He was blind with pain and definitely out of the fight with his blood spurting out between his fingers as he held his face. Dead-center impacts on the nose usually break the cartilage of the nose and that's extremely painful, especially for those who've just experienced it for the first time. Before another punch could be thrown, Bill spotted a police car across the street and he yelled "Cops!" Suddenly, Vern imagined the next news headlines, "Candidate for County Marshal Involved In Street Brawl". In a split second, Vern was off and running into the darkness, eventually loping about a mile south to a tavern that some of his friends frequented. As luck would have it, Charlie Lutkie was there and gave him a ride back to the gas station, well out of the danger zone. Meanwhile, Warfield leaned against his car with his arms folded and stubbornly held to his story, insisting to the policeman that he'd picked up a hitchhiker and didn't know his name (Bill's always been real good at holding a dead pan poker face).

Well, some days later, Bill walked into Vern's station and said "Vern, you'll never guess who's steam-cleaning pipe in that shop next door." Vern went to look and saw the guy he'd poked in the nose working diligently on that big pile of pipe. "Holy cow! That guy's huge! Bill, do you realize he coulda hurt me if he'd fallen on me? Man! Will ya look at those black eyes! His face is green and purple!"

The story didn't end there, either. Quite a few years later, Judge Paul Clark was visiting with Doug Irvin. Doug is now a retired policeman who works as a pre-sentence investigator for the District Court. Doug listened politely while Paul told the story and when he was finished Doug said, "Yeah Paul, I remember the incident real well because I was that cop and yes, I'd recognized Vern during the incident, but Warfield wouldn't budge from his story so I had no witness and had to let them go" ..and he rolled his eyes.

THE SEDGWICK COUNTY MARSHAL

Vern was ecstatic with his first big victory, so as soon as he took office he dove into the file drawers that were stuffed to overflowing with arrest warrants and wanted posters for everything from failure to pay parking tickets to murder and mayhem. His predecessor had left the office and assignments in a mess; the file cabinets looked like over-flowing wastebaskets. He remembers that it took a little while to arrange the work assignments, but it didn't take him long to figure out a system for spreading the workload that came out of those file cabinets. From there on he gave his Deputy Marshals a pep talk every day and they all went to work on the backlog with greatly renewed enthusiasm. The file cabinets emptied out within a few months, lots of old fines and their accompanying court costs were collected. More than just a few folks discovered that they could no longer hope that the Law would 'forget' them or that their little indiscretions might be buried in an overwhelming pile of bureaucratic paper. Quite a few of our good citizens soon discovered that any criminal warrant would set the Marshal's office in motion. The newly-discovered energy emanating from an office that had previously been very lethargic had an unexpected but predictable pay-off revealed in greatly renewed respect for our laws, legal system and lawmen. It wasn't a huge drop at first, but the crime rate began to take a noticeable downturn. The handwriting was on the wall, but few noticed.

While his crew was still busy cleaning up the mess left behind by their predecessors, Vern began looking around for more ways to occupy their time constructively. He really didn't like the image of running a department of doughnut-eating loafers, so he put considerable effort into changing it. Just about that time he noticed that other police departments periodically needed extra manpower and that they frequently had to use lots of unpaid overtime in order to get a job done. Typical of Vern, he didn't hesitate. He spread the word quickly among the other police departments to volunteer himself and his crew for mutual aid assistance, even for traffic control. The duty was good, but Vern and his crew soon found that they were far more interested in the investigation of criminal activity including undercover work. Again, their attitude was simply "Whatever it takes to get the job done, we'll do it." Rather than resenting the extra work and additional hazards, his Deputies found that they enjoyed the change of pace from the monotony of serving papers, making routine bench warrant arrests and escorting prisoners back to Wichita from other jurisdictions to face the music for their misdeeds. From some of these manpower loans, some of the deputy marshals and especially Vern, discovered that they had a real taste for undercover work. They honed it to a sharp edge over the years to come.

Not long after Vern took office it became apparent that there were sizeable differences between how Vern saw the Law and how Sheriff Denver Bland enforced it. It was most noticeable in the enforcement of our liquor laws; Vern's perception was very much in black and white. He didn't like or approve of the laxity of Bland's enforcement, so he went to the State Attorney General with evidence of liquor and gambling violations in and around Wichita. Vern had a small office with very little manpower and considering the political cronyism in the county at the time, Vern did an end-run around the sheriff and his buddy the county's prosecuting attorney to get the manpower he knew would be required. The Attorney General recognized the situation and immediately assigned several of the Assistant Attorneys General and a number of KBI officers to help. The raids were conducted, were quite successful, the sheriff's department was not notified in advance and news of it sent Sheriff Bland into orbit. Perhaps it was fortunate that he was very near his mandated term limit and couldn't run for the same office the very next year.

Left to right are Deputy Marshal Charlie Lutkie, Deputy County Attorney Guy Goodwin and MarshalVern Miller looking at a table loaded with liquor bottles from a raid on a club. This is one of the many incidents that sorely aggravated Sheriff Denver Bland and fomented considerable friction between Sheriff Bland and Marshal Miller. It was a running battle over jurisdiction and over how strictly the laws should be enforced. That battle ran for four years until both lost their re-election bids late in 1961.

Wichita Eagle Aug. 13, 1961

Every once in a while during his career Vern encountered a character who actually worked at developing a reputation for being solidly opposed to our laws; Marvin J. Igo was one such character. Marvin had a track record of jail escapes and was proud of being known as an escape artist, almost as proud as he was of his expensive shoes. Somehow he got crossways with the local law while Vern was Marshal, so once again he was booked into the County Jail. As he was being booked into jail he voiced what seemed like an innocent request that he be allowed to take his expensive leather shoes into his cell with him, which was an unusual request even considering the value of those shoes. Now because of Marvin's track record, that request set off alarms big time in Vern's head so he had those shoes inspected very thoroughly by Deputy Marshal Bill Warfield. Yes, that's 'Poker Face Bill' again. It didn't come as a great surprise when Bill found that hacksaw blades had been sewn between the layers of the leather soles and the escape attempt was foiled before it even got started.

Wichita Eagle Dec. 12, 1959
Inside Detective Magazine Mar., 1961

The first time we saw the picture of Vern appraising a crop of marijuana it was on the front page of the Wichita Eagle and the headline read "Marijuana 'Wholesaler' Nabbed in Topeka Raid". The next time we saw that same picture was over a year later where it was part of an entire article in a true crime magazine that had noticed some of Vern's accomplishments. The magazine article was entitled "Where The Poison Grass Grows Twelve Feet Tall" and it gave his political career quite a boost in addition to providing some very useful publicity for a problem he'd had with local law enforcement in our neighborhood for quite awhile.

The magazine that published that picture again was Inside Detective and it it caused them to get interested in what was going on in Kansas. When news got out that Vern, several of his deputies and a Wichita Police detective had been working undercover buying large amounts of marijuana from four pushers in Wichita, it really set the journalistic investigators into action. Here's a candid photo of Vern and Wichita Police Detective Melvin Rausch who went by the street name "Big 'Un".

What Vern and his peers really wanted was a direct line to the source of the marijuana flowing in Kansas and they finally found him, a major drug-dealer in Topeka. In order to even find him, it had taken quite a while to establish their undercover identities, cultivate the necessary contacts, get themselves introduced to the pushers and make the necessary purchases. Then they'd had to arrange the busts so they could lean on the pushers for information. As expected, some time after being arrested one of the pushers finally gave up the name of the supplier and Vern went to work to cultivate an acquaintance of the kingpin, Jack Jordan of Topeka. Again, it took a while, but Vern made the connection and cultivated the business relationship. Eventually Jordan revealed that he was getting much of his marijuana from a field on the Army base at Fort Leavenworth. During the investigation, Vern and Ray Bartholemew actually assisted Jordan in harvesting some marijuana and transporting it to Jordan's home to process it for sale. Finally, Vern called the Attorney General to advise him of what had developed from the operation and they coordinated a raid on Jordan's house. The time was ripe, so Vern and Ray went to the wholesaler, made a large purchase and the Attorney General's men busted Jack Jordan, seizing the entire inventory in the house in Topeka.

The Army wasn't aware of the problem crop until they heard it from the news media the following day. For security reasons, Vern and his team had not notified the Army of the operation, so Vern got his ear shredded on the phone the next day by the maddest Army Colonel he'd ever encountered. The Colonel was mostly aggravated because civil law enforcement had overlooked the courtesy of notifying base authorities about the illegal crop. Vern's pleasantly interested response to the Colonel's tirade was "Tough. Clean up your own back yard next time." The rest of the State's law enforcement agencies should've heeded all of this as a sign of things to come and maybe they did; maybe the seeds of the need for interdepartmental cooperation were germinating. Anyway, Vern shakes his head and grins about that phone call, but I'll bet he's just being diplomatically polite by refusing to talk about it.

Not only was that front page news article really bad press for the U.S. Army, upsetting U.S. base commanders around the world, it came as a major revelation to the public and the Kansas taxpayers were stunned! Collectively, their reaction was "What? It grows here? I thought that stuff came from Mexico!" Public reaction didn't end at the Kansas state line, either. You can bet that all military base commanders conducted site inspections real soon after the news broke.

Up to this time, the general public hadn't even been aware that the low potency, wild strain of marijuana is actually a weed that grows wild everywhere in all of the lower 48 states and Hawaii. But it came as quite a shock when we were told that the introduction of seeds for much higher potency, genetically-engineered pot was easy for local growers. Mother Nature's version is found where all weeds abound, in alleys, vacant lots, pastures, along roads and highways. The hot-rodded stuff that's cultivated and pampered really likes the company of sunflowers, corn and maize because of the fertilizer. In addition, it's frequently protected by its stewards so security from thieves and sharp-eyed police was and is usually accomplished by planting it in fields already planted in tall-growing crops. Sometimes there are hidden alarms and booby traps, too. Lots of parents in farming communities have been surprised to find that their youngsters and their friends had slipped a little extra seed into the soil, which in some states makes the property itself subject to confiscation. That revelation is never amusing to the owner-farmer and that news frequently comes from a friend who wears a badge, a guy that we pay to protect us from bad people.

Inside Detective Magazine Mar. 1961

Here's a press photo of Vern herding the members of his first big bust toward the courtroom from the jail.

The four had each sold narcotics to Vern while he was working undercover to find drug pushers and peddlers. Vern remembers that one of them was a U.S. Post Office employee and another was known on the street as Porkchop.

The picture above is in an album devoted to the period when most of Vern's time and energy was spent locating people who were wanted for crimes committed in Sedgwick County. Finding people who've gone down the wrong road can sometimes present quite a challenge for men and women that the taxpayers and bail bondsmen hire to do that job, but sometimes other people help. It's almost ironic that such outside help results from the habitual behaviors of the criminally inclined. Then and now, most tips that lead to arrests come from friends and family of the fugitives, but Vern's Deputies frequently discovered the whereabouts of people who were on the run from the law when their names would pop up on the hand-written and mail-delivered prison rosters like those from San Quentin and many others. The flaws in the system back then included a large gap in the time required to collect the information and then to get it published to the law enforcement people who needed it. It makes a great case for the instantaneous notification we have in today's computerized world where law officers nation-wide have up-to-the-minute news of who's in the slammer and the ability to compare fingerprints electronically is a phenomenal aid. Back in the early Sixties and before computers, one such fugitive was finally found in prison after he'd been wanted in Wichita for nine years. Today, even a routine traffic stop or getting tossed in a drunk tank triggers an automatic computer search of the "wants and warrants" system. Sometimes those searches result in phone calls to jails at the furthest reaches of the country with a "You've got him, we want him" and a "hold for extradition" which is known officially as a detainer, is put on the inmate. If the complaining department chooses, and they usually do, extradition procedures are set in motion and an officer will be sent to escort the prisoner back to face the music. In fact, many law officers spend most of their time on the road, often delivering one prisoner while enroute to picking up another. Our legal system spends a lot of money and manpower transporting bad people around the country with an escort to get their dose of justice.

Wichita Eagle Nov. 28, 1963

Early in Vern's first term as Marshal, the front-running Democratic candidate for President of the United States John F. Kennedy made a stop in Wichita and all law officers for miles in all directions were pressed into service to provide security because crowds of his fans were growing quite large by that time. Here's a photo of JFK in the center greeting the crowd of supporters with Vern in the lower right wearing a jaunty hat. If you look closely, you can see Vern guiding an adoring young boy's hand to touch the arm of the charismatic JFK's arm.

VOLUME IV NUMBER 48 PHONE MU 3-6531   NOVEMBER 28 1963 TWO SECTIONS

John F. Kennedy in Wichita in 1960

In the spring of 1961 during his tenure as Marshal, he decided to follow in his Uncle Alexander Miller's footsteps to become an attorney. At that time, the nearest school of law was located 150 miles south of Wichita where he lived and worked, so he faced a 300 mile roundtrip, three times each week for a total of 145,000 miles. It was a grueling challenge, but two years later he was joined by his friend Ray Hodge and several others in the pursuit of the title of attorney, so they carpooled most of the way and each of them wore out several cars in the process. They drove, hitchhiked, bummed rides with people they knew and some that they only met; they even flew a few times when Ray Hodge acquired a plane. The weather didn't show them any mercy and there were numerous mechanical failures, not to mention the highway construction zones that either slowed down their commute or re-routed them through detours. Vern finally graduated in 1966 while he was Sheriff and Ray graduated a year later while he was one of the Sheriff's captains. They'd been running in fast company during this phase of their education. By the time they graduated, they'd **become** the "fast company" and they were proud of it. As always, they were setting the bar progressively higher for the generations of those who followed them into law enforcement.

The mid-Fifties through the early Sixties was a period of technical advancements that set the stage for the computer age ranging from internal combustion engines to cosmetics, all costing money. One of the two popular forms of payment was of course cash and the other was personal checks. Well, a lot of folks with felonious inclinations found that the bank check system had several glaring flaws, so they began taking advantage of those flaws, mostly by "floating" checks between banks and then they'd simply disappear. But that was nothing compared to the big problem which quickly became known as "paper hanging" which was simply writing checks on accounts that either didn't exist or didn't have enough money in them to cover the string of checks coming in. Over a few short years, paper hanging became a serious problem for the banking industry and our economy. It quickly drove some small retail businesses into bankruptcy and even damaged a few large ones, but much worse than that was the impact that these problems had on the banking industry itself, which is the very backbone of our economy and the heart of our country's financial system.

Vern knew that he didn't have a magic bullet to solve the big problem, but the next best thing was to make the public aware of the problem and persuade the business community to tighten down their evaluations of their customers who asked to write personal checks for merchandise. As he'd said so often, "Bad people don't want publicity." He began distributing a weekly newsletter to local businesses listing the names that the bad check writers had used. It had a sudden and very measurable impact on the volume of these crimes. It was an extremely unusual approach, but it worked for as long as the effort was needed, which was as long as it took to plug the holes in the checking system nation-wide. Laws were quickly updated to clamp down hard on the paper hangers, giving them stiff sentences. Now this doesn't mean that his effort cleaned up the insufficient funds problem completely, but one of his many large scrapbooks is full of newspaper articles documenting the huge number of bad check writers that went to prison. The plague had been treated and the real vaccine was some very hard time sentences as the punishment for those criminals who were caught.

Sometimes some truly funny things happen during some otherwise serious events and Vern was involved in one one such while he was assisting in the search for an escapee from Sheriff Denver Bland's jail. Cops of all departments and jurisdictions were dispersed over the entire downtown area of Wichita and Vern decided to go inside a rather sleazy movie theater that was known as the Vogue Theater where the lowest levels of local society were known to gather for "entertainment". Naturally, Vern didn't want the clientele to know that there was a policeman among them, so after scanning the crowd on the ground floor he went upstairs to find the balcony nearly vacant, an ideal vantage point to watch the crowd. Soon after he sat down, a man appeared out of the darkness and instead of choosing to sit in the nearly 100 vacant seats available, he elected to sit down next to Vern. It didn't surprise Vern a few minutes later when he felt a hand on his knee, then it began to move slowly up his thigh. He didn't want to cause a ruckus or raise an alarm, in fact, he wanted to remain unnoticed, so he quietly pulled his pistol out of its holster and laid it across his lap because it was obvious that the hand would be going there next. Sure enough, the exploring hand arrived, discovered the pistol and the terrified stranger jumped out of that theater seat as though he'd sat on an electric fence. He actually ran down the dark stairway and was gaining speed as he went out the front door. So much for remaining invisible. Well, the jail escapee was caught anyway by another officer thirty minutes later over at the old Eaton Hotel, but Vern had gained another funny war story.

Shortly after he took office as marshal, Vern had formed the Vern Miller Boxing Team for the Boy's Club, passing on what he'd learned of the manly art of pugilism and attempting to keep at least some of the teenagers occupied and out of trouble. Quite a few of the boys learned their lessons well and went on to Golden Gloves competition which gained them considerable respect, something that's always been extremely important to teenaged boys on the verge of becoming men. Vern's very proud of them. The club was a viable entity from 1958 until he took office as the Attorney General in 1970 and then he had to move to be accessible to the State Capitol in Topeka.

Here's a photo of Vern holding a body bag while middle weight Alton Lane prepares to pound on it. Alton was very good; he had talent and Vern saw it. He encouraged Alton to study the sport and work hard to develop. Alton did and went on to win several Golden Gloves titles. After he retired from the sport he returned to his home town of Wichita to become a successful plumbing contractor, all of which makes Vern proud to talk about him. Alton Lane is just one of the many names that Vern reeled off and his pride in each of them was obvious. One of his remarks about the sport was something to the effect that it builds pride, self-confidence and that respect for others demands respect in return, which is a large step toward becoming an adult. He added that "Most of them were like I'd been as a youngster, high-risk kids from low income neighborhoods. Their self-esteem was in serious need of a boost, especially if it came from an authority figure that wanted to teach them something, anything that would help them improve their lot in life. Somehow, I knew that I had what they needed and I wanted to give it to them. They immediately showed that they really appreciated it. Most of them went on to be good citizens; I don't remember any of them going to jail for anything serious. As a matter of fact, two of the Hallacy brothers were among the members of the team we took into north Wichita to help quell the racial unrest in 1969 and '70. Very few of even the most rabid agitators challenged easy-going, laid-back Mike Hallacy when he told them to settle down and each of those who did quickly found out just how bad their judgement was. Mike was mellow and gentle, but taking a swing at him was about as smart as throwing a punch at a fast freight train and his brother Ned was a buzz saw with an easily-provokable attitude."

The old guy in the striped shirt is the teacher while the two youngsters just respectfully wish he'd quit talking so they can 'get it on.'

Wichita Eagle August 1, 1961

July 31st of 1961 was hot and muggy in Wichita, the District Court was in session, all normal for a workday in the courthouse. Then the unexpected happened. Vern and his Chief Criminal Deputy were working in the Marshal's office, unaware of what was about to happen. The seventh floor courtroom of Judge Clem Clark was jammed full of people waiting for divorce motions to be heard when suddenly a distraught husband drew a pistol and shot his newly-declared ex-wife dead. Then he turned the weapon and fired again, seriously wounding his ex mother-in-law right there in the courtroom. The crowd panicked and rushed hysterically out the doors and down the halls. There was utter pandemonium.

Judge Clem Clark immediately triggered the alarm which rang loud and frantically in the Marshall's office. Vern and Chief Criminal Deputy Ceasar DePascal dashed from the office and sprinted up the seven stories to the courtroom. Attorney Price Woodard met them as he was running down and yelled "Vern! He's got a gun!" As they ran toward the courtroom Vern yelled to Ceasar "Gimme your gun!" and Ceasar yelled back "I don't have it! It's back in the office!" Vern snapped "Ceasar, you're gonna get us both killed someday!" The two lawmen rushed into the courtroom unarmed and suddenly were face-to-face with an emotionally distraught gunman. Vern didn't hesitate; he pointed his finger at the man and shouted "Drop it or I'll kill you!" The gunman glanced at Vern and whether or not he realized that there was no gun in Vern's hand we'll never know. He shot and killed himself without hesitation. Judge Clark had frozen at the bench right where he sat. When Vern asked if he was alright, he answered shakily "I will be in a minute", whereupon he pulled a bottle of whiskey from a desk drawer and downed a huge gulp. Vern remembers that after the excitement had settled down that he thought glumly "Some days, there just are no victories."

Do you remember that Vern had been frustrated when as a young traffic cop he asked his superiors why something wasn't being done about the illegal drugs and the liquor violations? Well now he was in a position to do something about it. At the same time that he was cleaning out the backlog of fines owed to the taxpayers, he and his Deputies began cracking down hard on liquor violators and simultaneously they got into the illegal drug business by making purchases of illegal drugs and arresting the offenders. Although he sometimes played the part of a loner when he went undercover, he usually worked with one of his deputies. It just seemed the prudent thing to do for safety's sake and it worked like a charm, setting up one bust after another for the officers waiting just outside the door or around the corner. It was a pretty simple process, Vern or his partner would make the buy, then they'd leave and the other officers would step in to scoop up the drug dealer. He much preferred being in on the arrests, but for the sake of preserving his anonymity, he usually passed on the fun of making the arrests, although some were just too tempting to hand off to other members of his team.

Wichita Beacon Mar. 11 & 13, 1962

One such important arrest was that of a man known locally as a "big man" in the underground drug industry. This guy was a drug pusher named D.L. Sterling who seemed to have an endless supply of benzedrine. Vern figured that if he could come up with a plausible story that would pass him off as a college student with established "benny" customers, he might be able to deal with the big man himself. As it turned out, Vern's contrived image was so good that in only one phone conversation with D.L., he managed to gain an invitation to Sterling's house in Park City. He was posing as a college student from Oklahoma City who wanted a large quantity of "bennys" that he planned to retail. Sterling's wife met him courteously at the front door and made pleasant small talk as she led him to the kitchen to meet D.L.

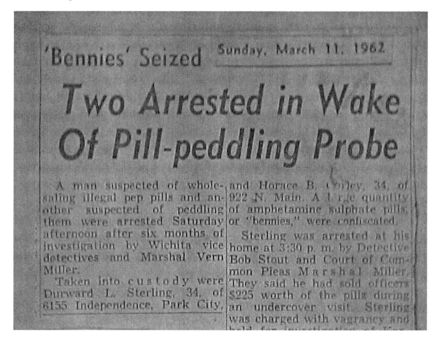

'Bennies' Seized   Sunday, March 11, 1962

Two Arrested in Wake Of Pill-peddling Probe

A man suspected of wholesaling illegal pep pills and another suspected of peddling them were arrested Saturday afternoon after six months of investigation by Wichita vice detectives and Marshal Vern Miller.

Taken into custody were Durward L. Sterling, 34, of 6155 Independence, Park City,

and Horace B. Worley, 34, of 922 N. Main. A large quantity of amphetamine sulphate pills, or "bennies," were confiscated.

Sterling was arrested at his home at 3:30 p. m. by Detective Bob Stout and Court of Common Pleas Marshal Miller. They said he had sold officers $225 worth of the pills during an undercover visit. Sterling was charged with vagrancy and

Vern didn't waste any time making the deal and left a few minutes later after trading cash for pills with D.L. The Wichita Detectives were sitting in their cars several blocks away and as Vern drove by them he slowed enough to tell them that the deal had gone down. The Wichita Police been after D.L. for quite some time with little success, so they happily went off to arrest Mr. Sterling while Vern went back to being the County Marshal. It'd been a good day for all except, of course, for D.L. Sterling.

One of Sterling's retailers (pushers) was Horace B. Corley and the Wichita Police caught up with him several hours later for selling some bennys to undercover policemen. Sterling and Corley each served a year in jail and paid fines, plus suffering the indignity of the public chewing from an irate Judge Robert Morrison who was known to have a hard mouth, sharp teeth and a burning temper for criminals and miscreants.

There were quite a few liquor violation cases in critical places about the same time, so the message was getting out that these were two types of crimes that'd seen their day and would no longer be ignored, overlooked or protected. Although Vern was stepping on the toes of some of the other agencies pretty hard by tightening up the acceptable rules of behavior, the press kept the spotlight of public attention on him, refusing to allow those other agencies to slow him down or retaliate behind the scenes. The news media, especially the Wichita Eagle, deserves a sincere round of applause for that. Although it's taken some of us decades to figure it out, the Eagle has long been a moral tentpole in the community. One small example of this is that the Eagle occasionally hired a rooky reporter from out of town to snoop out where liquor was being sold illegally, then the rooky was told by his editor to take the list to Miller for his comment. That rooky was surprised and disappointed that Vern barely acknowledged it as he accepted the list, but the young reporter was delighted when he learned that all of the businesses on the list were raided and busted poste haste, even though the articles as written by the rooky never ran in the newspaper. There are no finite figures available, but it appears that there were far more drug busts and liquor violations busts during Vern's first year as marshal than there'd been in the entire county for the previous ten years.

Then came a large dose of humility. Vern's huge fan club wasn't paying attention at election time and many of us failed to make it to the polls that year so he lost his bid for election as Sheriff in 1962. A succession of other jobs followed, but none of them were in law enforcement. None of them were very satisfying, but they paid the rent and Vern bided his time until the next election.

THE SEDGWICK COUNTY SHERIFF

This time he had a strong foothold in the Democratic Party plus serious name recognition along with a proven track record. Once again he used his boundless energy and enthusiasm, this time to run hard for the office of Sheriff in 1964. The press already knew and loved the colorful candidate and the Democratic Party recognized a winner when they saw one, so they got behind him to get his name and face in front of the voting public. His campaign schedule would have exhausted a lesser candidate. He talked to absolutely everybody beginning early in the morning in the coffee shops until late at night, one-on-one or any group that would listen and he told them all repeatedly of the increasing drug problem and the accompanying crime rate that was soaring. The voters remembered the vigorous Miller and this time we re-joined his crusade, welcoming him back to public service with open arms and a resounding victory. We did it two more times after that, too. It's definitely worth noting that from that point on, voter turnout was always much higher when Vern Miller was on the ticket because of his enthusiasm, his sincerity and the loyalty of his admirers. Although we were skeptical at the time, he relentlessly reminded us that each of us has more than just a right to vote, we have a responsibility to vote!

He was back in law enforcement and his commitment was stronger than ever because he'd been watching the news with increasing concern and the media was telling us about increasing drug activities in and around Wichita. Meantime, the drugs were still overflowing from Lawrence, Manhattan and Leavenworth into neighboring communities, including Vern's jurisdiction and it quickly became a challenge so he went to work right after his election implementing his campaign promise to come down hard on drugs. Time after time, the drugs scooped up in busts in Wichita and Sedgwick County had the earmarks of having come from the other big college towns even though Wichita State University had a sizeable student population of its own. Talking to the various police departments in those other jurisdictions always brought words of sympathy, promises to crack down, even more promises to cooperate in shutting off the supply, but Vern saw no measurable improvement. The thought that kept going through his mind was that "This is going to stop if I have to go plug the pipeline myself!" Ultimately he did just that, but at the time he lacked the authority and resources to fight the drug war on two fronts even though he knew the source of the contraband pouring into his county.

Since illegal drug habits costs the drug users increasingly larger amounts of money, sooner or later they inevitably run out of money of their own so they turn to stealing to support their habits. Family members, friends and neighbors all feel the effect as thefts of anything convertible to cash increases radically and families are frequently their first targets. The victims of the thefts nearly always notify the police and insurance companies so the costs to all of us begin to mount, but the thief is rarely named so he or she is still free to continue both the habit and the crimes. Then the stolen contraband starts turning up in flea markets, yard sales and pawn shops for hundreds of miles in all directions, making the job of finding and retrieving it extremely difficult if not impossible, but the pattern exposes what drives the thefts. Based on the increased numbers of treatment for overdoses and deaths from them, the emergency room personnel confirmed that the causes driving the theft patterns were drug abuse and many of those victims were on welfare, so the taxpayer was also taking a hit.

A lot of things were happening all at the same time, so we'll continue to list them as chronologically as possible. Vern had just taken office as sheriff for the first time and since it was the way of the times back in those days, he completely re-staffed his new department beginning with a new command staff. He certainly realized that he needed a better head jailer than his predecessor had left in place, so one of the first things Vern did was to reach into the ranks of his very competent friends to tap Charlie Lutkie on the shoulder, offering him the job. Charlie had some rather unique qualifications that Vern admired greatly, most notably that Charlie had once been crowned the light-heavyweight champion professional wrestler of the Central Division, definitely not a guy to mess with. He was also a licensed professional boxer, the only man in history to own both licenses simultaneously in the state of Kansas. Viewing this in retrospect, I'd say that this was probably another sign of unpleasant things to come for our criminal element.

Well, Charlie was a humble guy who'd never thought of himself as "the boss", so he wanted to think about it awhile. Rather than let his perfect candidate make a wrong decision, Vern took Charlie on a tour of the jail and one of the inmates played right into Vern's game plan by yelling derisively "Hey, Shurff. Who's th' lil fat guy?" and followed that with more wisecracks that aren't fit for mixed company. Charlie must've been sensitive about his weight that day and the heckling irritated him so much that he took the job on the spot. Sure enough, a few days later Charlie validated his new boss's choice a when a little ruckus broke out in the hallowed halls of the ol' County jailhouse. The no-holds-or-punches-barred brawl lasted for almost twenty minutes and Charlie Lutkie was the last man standing. The upshot of this episode was that the word got around town quickly that the Sedgwick County Jail was a poor place to misbehave.

Mike Danford

Wichita Eagle May 29, 1965

Shortly after Vern was elected, two county jail inmates escaped and although one of them was soon back in custody, the other remained on the loose. It was the second successful escape for Richard Lee McCarther, who had been waiting to be transferred to prison to serve a total of 119 years for a total of ten felonies including armed robberies. The duo had managed to escape from the county jail by removing a steel door that provided access to the plumbing, crawled into the attic. Then they worked their way to the jailhouse outer wall, pried a safety screen from a window and climbed seven stories down a rope made of sheets tied together. It'd been quite an athletic feat, but Vern didn't appreciate it because he was openly sensitive about the security of the jail he'd inherited. The intense search was focussed on Wichita and was tightly centered around Mac's wife who had warned police vehemently that Mac wouldn't go back to jail, that "You're not going to take him now. He'll kill you first." That sort of threat doesn't intimidate lawmen; it just makes them very edgy.

It took several months for word to get to Vern that Mac might have made his way to Omaha and was probably living with friends up there. Without waiting for the proper protocols, Vern grabbed Deputy Sheriff Clay Cox and drove north, convinced that he had a hot lead.

During the six hour drive, the thought kept running through Vern's mind that there had to be a reason for Mac being in Omaha and suddenly he had it. He remembered that used car dealer Jim Earp, a former Wichitan, had bought a Chrysler dealership in Omaha and that MacArther's fall partner had worked for Earp several years earlier in Wichita. At that point, Vern surmised that the other lot boys might know of Mac's whereabouts so Vern called Jim and asked him if he'd taken any employees with him to Omaha from Wichita. Jim said he had two from Wichita so Vern arranged to drive to Omaha to meet Jim to get the addresses of those two employees.

When Vern and his deputy arrived, Jim insisted that they use a car from his lot because even an un-marked police car would quickly be spotted in the black section of town. Then Vern went to talk to the Omaha Police who were surprised when they arrived on such short notice. Omaha had very little manpower available at that moment, but they assigned a couple of aging detectives to assist. The two detectives didn't look like they'd be much help, but Vern was anxious to get on with the search so he took what he could get.

They'd hardly made it into the neighborhood where Mac was rumored to be living when Vern spotted Mac walking along the sidewalk wearing a pair of Bermuda shorts and carrying a small bundle of laundry. Mac recognized them immediately, dropped the bundle and took off running as soon as the car stopped. Deputy Cox jumped out of the car and immediately fired two warning shots in the air hoping to stop the fleeing MacCarther, then he took off running to cut off one route of escape. Vern was out of the car and running as hard as he could after Mac. He was in hot pursuit, adrenaline pumping, pulse pounding in his ears and gun in hand because a shootout was expected; Vern remembered vividly the words of Mac's wife that "He'll kill you first!" Mac was fast on his feet and knew the territory, so it was a long, three-block chase, zigzagging through back yards, parking lots and vacant lots. Realizing that Mac had the advantage and might escape, Vern finally fired two quick shots, one which grazed Mac from behind through the side of his upper lip. The concussion of the near-miss knocked Mac off-stride and he flipped as he went to the ground, but he was quickly up again and running. Vern had gained considerably in that brief moment and was now right on his heels. Mac tried to climb a tall fence and was attempting to climb over when Vern grabbed his foot, pulled him down and the chase was over, but now the fight was on, the trained welterweight against the lean and wiry street fighter. Mac was no slouch and had a lot to lose, so it wasn't your average brawl; it was real serious for both of them! Vern remembers doing a little trash-talking, grinning at Mac while they were swapping punches. He growled "Mac, I love ya, ya sonovabitch, but you're going home!" Vern can't remember if Mac responded, but if he did, you can bet that it wasn't nice. Deputy Cox arrived from a different route and angle, but when he got there, the wrestling/slugging match with the desperate McCarther was over and Miller was sitting on top of Mac. They got the handcuffs on quickly, but that's when they found that a crowd had gathered around them in an ugly mood and the blood-soaked Mac was beaten, furious, still spitting and fuming and egging the crowd on.

With Mac's blood splashed all over them and dripping from both Vern and Mac, they moved slowly to the curb from a back yard with the threatening crowd growing while the emotional temperature of the crowd climbed rapidly. Among the many other thoughts they were screaming "Let him go!" The mob followed them while the trio made their way back to the street to wait for the detectives and the car. Conditions were rapidly approaching being very ripe for a full-blown race riot. The mood of the crowd was ugly, getting worse by the minute and the air became so loaded with venomous electricity that Vern and the Deputy drew their guns again to make it clear that they meant to protect themselves and their prisoner with deadly force if necessary. In the verbal exchange with the rabid hecklers, Miller and Cox made sure that they left no doubt that they intended take their prisoner to jail at all costs, even if the crowd attacked. The atmosphere was extremely tense for a few minutes, but nobody in the angry crowd was willing to challenge the blood-soaked lawman's determination when Vern pointed his pistol at them and barked "The first one that steps off that curb is gonna die!" The belligerent crowd stayed on the curb, but they began throwing bottles and rocks at the three in the street.

The two Omaha detectives arrived with the car just in the nick of time, picked up the trio and went straight to the Omaha jail, the bottles and rocks bouncing off the car as they left the scene. After Mac was securely tucked into a jail cell, the borrowed car was taken back to Jim Earp. While Vern and Clay were there, they interviewed the Earp's two employees who had been close to MacCarther. It didn't take long to get one of them to admit that Mac had intimidated him, forced him to let him hide in his house and that he'd seen Mac with a gun in his bedroom. A quick trip to the house produced a loaded .45, lending considerable credence to Mac's wife's statement that "He'll kill you first" rather than surrender peacefully.

MacCarther refused to waive extradition to the state of Kansas, so the lawmen returned to Wichita to find a big celebration party waiting for them at the County courthouse. A few days later after extradition was completed, Mac was taken straight to the penitentiary at Lansing.

Pictured left to right are Deputy Sheriff Clay Cox, MacCarther and Sheriff Miller.

Mac's escape had been a rude awakening that the hinges on the locks installed on the jail's plumbing doors hadn't been made of hardened steel to prevent being sawed through. It also pointed out that that there wasn't enough manpower to seal off the County with roadblocks which prompted Vern to go to work on enlarging the Sheriff's Reserve, a standing posse of commissioned officers. Once the word got out of the need, there was no shortage of willing and qualified volunteers. The officers that he commissioned were unpaid, strictly volunteer citizens who were willing to donate their time and services for a very worthy cause. They furnished their own guns, badges and uniforms, then they were given their assignments for whatever time they were able to donate. At its peak, the Reserves Unit numbered over 150 and Vern says that when the order was given, all roads in and out of Sedgwick County were being blockaded within a few minutes. During one such exercise, a man who was wanted for a murder 30 miles south of Wichita in Wellington was caught. Just a few weeks later those same roadblocks caught 7 of the 12 escapees after the biggest jailbreak in the history of this state and nobody got hurt. That's not at all bad for a civil militia.

Wichita Beacon June 13, 1968

Bernie Ward wrote the article that told readers about a typical day in the life of an active sheriff. He described one 24-hour period in Vern's life that began with:

"Went north to quell a family disturbance and subdue a man armed with a loaded shotgun and a loaded .22 caliber pistol.

Went southeast to set up a widespread dragnet and direct the capture of four burglary and auto theft suspects.

Went west to Lake Afton to rush a drowning victim to St. Francis Hospital in a frantic race against death.

In between these emergencies Miller attended a meeting with the Sedgwick County Commissioners and the County Fire Chief; answered incessant phone calls from officers, citizens and civic leaders, advised staff members who streamed in and out of his office and managed to sit quietly – an uncharacteristic pose – and discuss the complexities of his job."

"It was nearly midnight Wednesday, 24 hours after his day began, that Miller finally went home to bed."

Remember that this was described as a "typical" day, not as any kind of an exception and it was for a 24 hour period rather than an 8 hour day at the office. The phenomenal stamina required to maintain this pace for the six years in office served him and his constituents extremely well and would continue to do so for years to come. He was indefatigable, often working several consecutive shifts and exhausting his subordinates, frequently forcing him to send some of them home to sleep.

Wichita Beacon July 12, 1968
(front page) Detective Magazine Oct. 1968

People who take a wrong turn down life's road frequently continue that pattern and unfortunately, sometimes it results in progressively violent behaviors. Following their felonious tracks back in time, they can usually be traced back to where they made that first bad decision. Such was the case for four such characters, two in particular. Marvin Fisher and Richard Sargent were suspected of having robbed and murdered a well-liked farmer in southwest Missouri, 74-year-old bachelor Edwin Frey. The murder was brutal; the victim had been handcuffed to a chair and shot in the head three times.

The trail was still very warm as it led down into Fayetteville, Arkansas where the group had abandoned their car in a parking lot. From there, they'd boarded a Continental Trailways bus bound for Denver with their female companions. The Sheriff in charge of the crime scene in Newton County Missouri quickly found that the route of the bus included Wichita, then he called ahead hoping to head them off. The phone call from Sheriff Forrest (Frosty) Land in Neosho alerted Sheriff Miller that trouble was on the way, so he pulled Traffic Sgt Darrel Schooler, Detective Ed Miller and Detective Art Stone from the support for a drug bust in progress. The brief telephone conversation with Frosty set Vern and his team in motion, moving quickly to intercept the bus as far outside the crowded core of the city as possible. The fast-moving lawmen barely accomplished that. They met the bus and stopped it just north of MacArthur and Broadway, right in front of Warne's Flower Shop at 12:26 a.m. on that hot, muggy, June night.

The groggy and innocent passengers didn't know why the bus had stopped, but they could see the flashing beacons on the police cars and the uniforms, so they knew it was something serious. It made the fugitives uneasy because they suspected what was happening and why, but only one of them was ready and determined to put up a fight. As the driver stepped off the bus he was informed that he might have a killer on board and he immediately volunteered to go down the aisle first to make it appear that nothing was wrong, reassuring the passengers as he went. It sounded like a good plan, so Vern left two officers outside to guard the door while he, the bus driver and Detective Art Stone climbed aboard. The three of them walked down the aisle slowly toward the back of the bus, looking each passenger in the face as they went. They were past the halfway point when Vern noticed a male passenger sitting next to the aisle with a khaki shirt covering his hands. Vern quietly asked him for identification, but instead the suspect whipped out a loaded snd cocked .44, vintage revolver from under the khaki shirt and tried to point it at Vern. Time is measured in tenths, hundredths, even thousandths of a second in life-or-death situations with several things happening simultaneously and this was one of those times. Within the space of far less than one second, Vern simultaneously hit him in the face and grabbed the gun arm, shoving it down and away, holding it there with all the strength he had. The bus driver reacted almost as quickly and wrapped his arm around the man's head and face, pulling it back so he couldn't see where the gun was pointed. Fisher was lean, strong and wiry and was nowhere near being under control with that weapon in his hand and leverage in his favor.

Detective Lt. Art Stone had been walking carefully five feet behind Vern when he saw the action erupt, so all in one motion he whipped out his pistol and shot the suspect dead-center in the chest, killing Fisher instantly. The fatal bullet passed just inches beneath Vern's right arm. Seconds later, there was a very brief struggle with Sargent, who had suddenly decided to join the fray when the enormous sound of the gunshot in such close quarters jarred him into action. He scrambled to reach a loaded rifle that was rolled up in a blanket lying on the floor, but he didn't even get close to it before Vern and Art were on him. Watching their friend die violently right in front of them had stunned the other three momentarily, probably delaying their reactions just enough. Vern was immediately on the floor wrestling with Sargent and Stone was angling to assist when Detective Ed Miller and Sgt. Schooler arrived just in time to intercede to prevent one of the women from using a .22 automatic pistol she'd pulled out of her purse. After that, there was no further resistance. The deadly confrontation was over. The example had been set. Threaten a police officer with a gun and the use of deadly force is not only justified, it'll probably be used.

Along the dead killer's trail were a seven-year prison sentence and a string of lesser crimes in several other states where he was wanted for questioning. For all of the policemen and the bus driver involved in the incident, it had been part of their jobs to protect the innocent from the criminal element of our society, especially violent criminals. For Marvin Fisher's three partners in crime, there was only extradition to Missouri and jail sentences remaining.

Art Stone is a large, easy-going, thoughtful man who chooses his words carefully and when I asked him recently how he made the decision to shoot Marvin Fisher so quickly, he looked at me levelly and responded without hesitation. "There was no decision to make and no time to make one anyway. A man with a gun was trying to kill my friend and I couldn't allow that, so

I reacted instinctively." That's a very candid quote from a very strong, very loyal lawman.

This photo shows Vern assisting in the loading of Marvin Fisher onto a gurney after Detective Art Stone shot him.

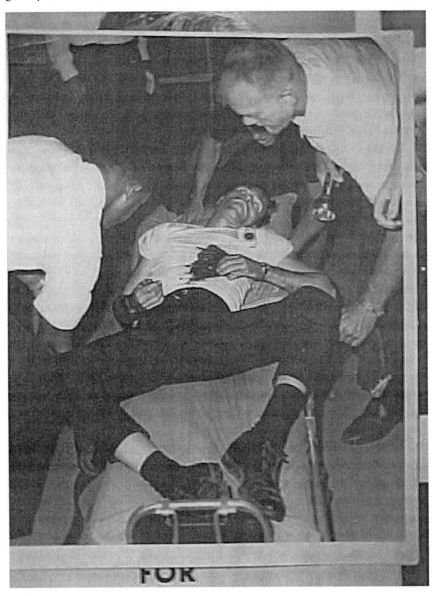

Vern's brother, Army Col. Dan Miller was home on leave and had been riding with Vern just to spend time with his little brother. Dan had been waiting patiently outside the bus while the action progressed inside, fully aware that it was a potentially dangerous situation. He said later that he knew immediately that Vern was alright after the gunshot was heard when he heard his younger brother's gravelly voice shout excitedly "Boy, Stone! I sure hope this is the right sonuvabitch!"

That's the pistol that Marvin Fisher tried to use to kill Sheriff Miller, right where it landed on the floor. Notice that the deadly .44 caliber pistol is still loaded and cocked. The toe of Detective Art Stone's boot is shown at the upper left.

That's the story of what happened and where, when and how. What followed isn't recorded anywhere that I know of, but I managed to get some of the pieces by listening closely to some of the people who had been there. Art Stone had reflexively pulled the trigger to protect his friend and he was the one who reflected thoughtfully to me some forty years later that "The gun that every law enforcement officer carries is his tool of absolute last resort… and every single one of us prays that we never, **ever** have to use that tool."

It's obvious that there's a price to pay for even witnessing the violent taking of a human life even to prevent harm to another human, much less actually participating in it. I could see it in the discussions on the subject with Vern. During the many conversations with him about this particular episode and its after-effects, I noticed that he seldom realized that what he was describing were numerous periods of gloom and depression that had followed the event. He described the classic symptoms of sudden feelings of frustrated anger, often followed by feelings of hopelessness that man will ever change for the better.

The world of psychology and psychiatry was still on the brink of discovering the consequences of such tragedies, so there was no established procedures for treating the victims until many years later. However, I've been told that we know now that there are only two solutions for this type of injury. The first, which was known at the time and somewhat explains what drove Vern, is the total distraction provided by familiar work at hand. The other has been discovered and developed within the last thirty years, is by use of professional counseling that forces talking about it, working through it, much like washing laundry by hand, one piece at a time. Either or both of these solutions only minimize the impact of the emotional trauma, but neither makes it go away completely and only time will heal the wound and the emotional scars will remain for a lifetime.

Wichita Eagle Mar. 1, 1970

A fella named Don Gasser (remember this name 'cause it'll come up again later) wound up being held in the Sedgwick County Jail on an arrest warrant from California for robbery. Now Don was a big, muscular, ruggedly good-looking guy, sorta like Nick Nolte in his prime and he came across as being easy-going, funny and friendly. He was articulate and glib, but if anybody had told him he wasn't smart enough to make a living being a criminal without getting some free room and board now 'n then he wouldn't have believed it. We know now that his sense of criminal mischief was exceptionally creative and always self-serving. Before the marshal from California arrived to escort Gasser back for prosecution for his crime, Don engineered a way out of the jail and led twelve prisoners in the biggest jailbreak in the history of Sedgwick County and the State of Kansas. Seven of them were recaptured that night while driving stolen cars that same night, all at roadblocks that'd been set up by Miller's volunteer Reserve Unit. One gave himself up a day later, Gasser was at large for almost two weeks and the remainder of the escapees were eventually captured.

Wichita Eagle Feb. 26, 1970

One of these escapees was Isaiah Rhone who was considered to be very dangerous since he had a history of running from law officers, burglary, hit-and-run and was suspected of frequently carrying a gun. Rhone was big, fast, strong and he had a record of violence, which is why he was thought to be so dangerous. The jailbreak was four days old when an anonymous tip got to Vern that Rhone had been hiding from the law in a girlfriend's apartment on East 17th Street.

Our laws of legal entry for pursuit of lawbreakers were still unrefined to the point of requiring a search warrant at that time, so Sheriff Miller, Johnny Darr and Detective Ross Greenfeather barged into the apartment over the strenuous objections of the two women who opened the door. Ross followed the two women into the kitchen when one of them yelled "Get the gun!" while the sheriff and his second-in-command sprinted straight to the bedroom. At first glance when they viewed the room, all they saw were several startled children whose sleep had been interrupted. However, closer observation revealed that there were two very large bare feet showing beneath the clothes hanging in the closet. Flashlight in hand, Vern went to the closet and jerked the clothes out of the way, which brought Isaia lunging out and grabbing Vern's flashlight right out of his hand enroute. Vern anticipated the next move, so he ducked and drove his fist into Isaia's mid-section just as Isaia swung the flashlight downward. It had been meant for Vern and there was a lot of force behind it, but it caught Johnny Darr squarely on top of his head and knocked him unconscious for the next several minutes. It wasn't just a little bonk and it'd dropped him cold, so Darr wasn't at his best even when he regained consciousness several minutes later and he had a serious headache for awhile. Meantime, Vern and Isaia were swapping vicious punches and wrestling around the room, falling on the bed among and on top of several very excited children. Greenfeather had finally secured his charges with handcuffs, so he arrived to help Vern and the verrry groggy Darr install handcuffs on Rhone, then haul the still-raging and struggling Rhone outside to a waiting car to take him back to jail. The two women were arrested the next day on charges of harboring a fugitive. Just in case you were concerned about those children, none of them were hurt, but they had a very exciting story to tell their friends.

Jail Escapee Battles Officers in Attempt To Avoid Recapture

FEB 2 6 1970

By BERNIE WARD
Beacon Staff Writer

One of four Sedgwick County jail escapees fought recapture when Sheriff Vern Miller and two detectives found him

IN OTHER developments today Attorney Robert Roth has authorized filing of a federal complaint charg two of the escapees, Eugene F. Gen 41, and Eugene Littlejohn, 22, escaping federal custody.

Meantime, Gasser had been out for over a week and the last remaining escapee evaded arrest for several more years, but eventually the long arm of the law snagged every one of them. Donny wasn't the last one caught even though he was on the run lots longer than most of the escapees.

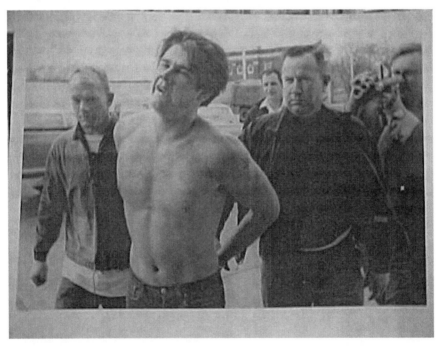

Although this picture and the accompanying article seems to have run in nearly every newspaper in the state, I got it from an article in the Wichita

Eagle who openly supported our aggressive lawman. Left to right in the foreground is Sheriff Miller, Don Gasser (shirtless and handcuffed), future Sheriff Johnny Darr, Detective Ernie Feeler and KTVH-TV cameraman Bill Tippets. Gasser was caught because Vern knew that Donny's girlfriend had been charged with burglary and that the charge was still pending. In order to gain her cooperation, Vern promised to help her try to get the charge reduced if she would help him capture Gasser. Since she was the sole support of two small children, she was really anxious to get any help she could, promising her full support and cooperation. Sure enough, several nights later she called Vern at home from the nightclub where she worked to tell him that Donny had called, asked her to meet him one more time before he left for California and she'd accepted. She told Vern that Donny was hiding in a house next door to the Old Waterhole Club just west of the already infamous Rock Castle Club on north Broadway and he'd instructed her to park her car in the nightclubs' parking lot, then walk the short distance to the house.

It was an interesting arrest for several reasons; there were some tactical challenges in addition to some physical obstacles and then there was the eternal screw-up lurking. First, the entire street had to be quietly blocked off so as to avoid alerting Donny or his lookouts. Then there were two or three big, apparently vicious German Shepherds that had to be neutralized with Mace before the officers could even get into the yard and it had to be done so in a hurry so that the policemen could hit the door quickly. Next, there were several other people in the house in addition to the fugitive, so the unforeseen introduced a confusion factor, which played a big part. Thus, after several hours of evaluating the situation and planning the finite details of the assault in a cold and miserable rain, it was time to launch. Vern gave the order to launch the operation and almost immediately it became apparent that there'd been a small glitch in the plan. Vern ran to the back door alone and nobody covered the bedroom window while second-in-command Johnny Darr and the rest of the entire team of officers went to the front door of the house. The front and back doors were breached simultaneously, alerting Gasser who quickly pulled on his pants as he went barefoot out a window on the back side of the house with Vern diving out the same window right on his heels. Each of them tumbled as they hit the ground and both came up running, but Vern had the distinct advantage of sprinter speed. It was a half mile foot race followed by a brief wrestling match that ended when Detectives Ernie Feeler and Roy Rains arrived to pile on and force the handcuffs on the struggling Gasser.

Describing that incident, Vern said with a grin, "Aw, we weren't mad at him. But we'd been hiding out there in the rain all night, so the whole team was cold, hungry, tired and sorta inspired to wrap it up. Donny was fresh from a good night's sleep, but he hadn't had breakfast either so we stopped at a pancake house on the way to the jail and everybody except Donny felt much better after a hot meal. He was still a little grouchy about being caught when we arrived at the jail, so he took a wild kick at (TV cameraman) Bill Tippets, but he missed and we got him inside without further incident."

One of the other prisoners who'd been recaptured needed some medical attention, so Vern and Captain Lutkie had taken him to St. Francis Hospital. While they were in the Emergency Room, Charlie noticed a man lying on a stretcher. The man's clothes were ripped and torn, he had numerous painful injuries and he was obviously very drunk. Charlie exclaimed "Hey! That's one of our escaped prisoners!" Sure enough, closer examination revealed that the moaning, fumey character was indeed one of the men they'd been searching for and when he recognized Charlie his first words were "God, am I glad to see you guys!"

The following story soon unfolded. Following the breakout he'd run south on Broadway, right into what was then the Old Mule Train Inn where a private party was in full swing. Realizing that his best cover was a crowd, he joined the party in progress with a bunch of cowboys and immersed himself in free beer until the cowboys realized that he was not one of them. Well, the rowdy cowboys were juiced up and ready to play, so they bounced him around some before they ejected him rather unceremoniously, so he wound up lying in the middle of the street where he was soon hit by a taxicab. The cab driver reported the accident to the police through his dispatcher, but before the police arrived the drunk had staggered off into a nearby yard where a very territorial Chow dog punished him for trespassing. Police arrived, talked the big Chow into a truce and provided the drunk with an ambulance ride to the emergency room for a lot of patching, stitching and disinfecting, which of course is where Capt. Lutkie spotted the luckless guy.

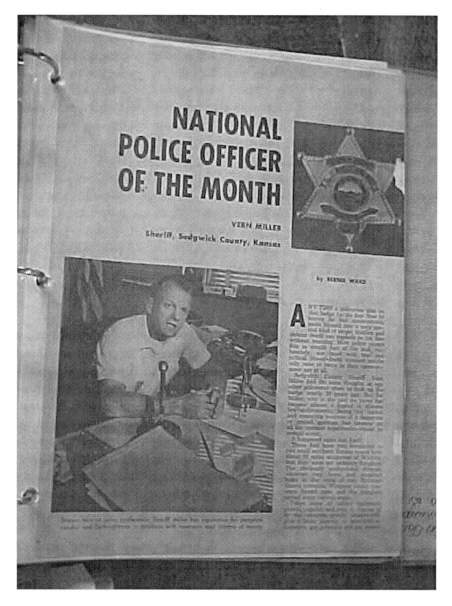

The news media has always been an extremely powerful entity and it's certainly had its darlings down through the ages. Some of those darlings have been flashes in the publicity pan, others have somehow gone sour while some have proven to be emerging icons of their trade like some of our professional athletes vaulting from the amateur ranks into stardom. Mohammed Ali of boxing fame is one good example and George Foreman is another, Babe Ruth is legendary while football players Joe Montana, John Elway and hockey player Wayne Gretsky all made their way to the top of their professions, just to name a very few. Then for other achievements not necessarily of their choosing there are many that we admire and applaud who are suddenly thrust into the limelight of world news unwillingly. One good example locally is PFC Patrick Miller of Valley Center when he was a POW held by hostile Iraqi forces; not so local is the venerable Senator John McCain of Arizona who was a POW of the North Vietnamese Army for six long years. But Vern's never been held against his will. He actually sought public office, so he more accurately resembles real life hero FBI Agent Elliot Ness of "The Untouchables" fame in more than a few ways. He was then and is now soft-spoken, reasonable, self-assured and like Ness, he's the classic "straight arrow" except that, unlike the poker-faced Ness, he has an infectious grin to match his enormous energy. In their issue of October, 1970 Master Detective magazine chose Vern the National Police Officer of the Month, which is quite an honor for any policeman.

Wichita Eagle June 6, 1967

Because we're all human, each of us occasionally reaches a point where normal daily stresses build to a low-level climax. Most of our emotional apexes are relatively minor, requiring only a temper tantrum, some vigorous physical exercise to work off the emotional steam or perhaps something similar to few hours of fishing to smooth it out. Once in a while, however, other pressures are added to our daily ration until they build past the danger point and something snaps, resulting in major emotional crises that require medical help in order to bring them safely under control. This latter situation is a bit like a nuclear melt-down in that once critical mass is reached, about all the rest of us can do is try to protect each other until the explosion is past, so we try to do our best to defuse these episodes. This next situation is a very good example of one such stress over-load.

Emotionally overwrought people frequently present law officers with pretty serious challenges and in June of 1967, one of those happened. For Vern, this incident started when the Sheriff's dispatcher received a call that sent Vern, Detective John Hale and many other officers racing through the driving rain of a thunderstorm in the dark, hoping to head off a suicide attempt. As they approached the neighborhood of the woman in trouble, word came over the radio that her car had been found abandoned near I-235 and Old Lawrence Road, so Vern and John went there and began looking around in the darkness for the most likely place she might be. Sure enough, they found her crouching under a nearby tree with a pistol in her hand, dripping wet, cold, disheveled and hysterically paranoid.

After several failed attempts, Vern and John were finally able to get close enough to talk to her calmly and patiently, even though she alternated between pointing the gun at them and then at herself. Her hysteria surged and waned as her energy level fluctuated and she claimed among other things that she was married to a holder of the Congressional Medal of Honor and that she was being tortured by her burning love for an ex-convict. The howling wind, pouring rain and darkness made much of what she said unintelligible and probably exacerbated her hysteria, but it was obvious that she was in severe distress that was accelerating. She was moaning, crying and threatened repeatedly to kill herself, but they kept her talking long enough that her need for nicotine finally led to John offering her a cigarette. Vern knew that John was setting her up, so he was ready when she reached for the cigarette. With split second timing, he grabbed her while John grabbed the gun. Suddenly, the crisis was over. It'd been a very long thirty minutes for the two lawmen, but the incident had ended with no one hurt.

**Wichita Eagle August 4, 1967 February 28, 29 March 15, 17, 1968
Wichita Beacon February 26, 27, 1968**

Dan Canfield of the Wichita Crime Commission and Bill Tippet, KTVH-TV photographer were riding with Vern the night of August 3, 1968 because the level of racial tension was mounting over the civil rights issues when this took incident place. Racial tensions are always a problem for police since they're supposed to be in a neutral position, yet they're always caught in between the opposing factions and charged with the responsibility for keeping the peace. Sometimes it's difficult to hear or even think when groups of people are busy screaming and yelling at each other with the peacekeeper between them trying to keep tempers from flaring.

Vern, Canfield and Tippet were sitting in a dark blue, unmarked sedan talking amiably with a large group of black teenagers late one evening about an earlier incident when a car with five white youths stopped at the intersection of 13th and Hydraulic about fifty yards away. One of the white youths stepped out of the car and fired at the group hitting three of the black teenagers and Vern with the lightweight birdshot. There were no serious injuries because of the fairly short effective range of the lightweight shot, but it was an attack with a firearm. The car carrying the white youths was a factory hotrod, a 396 Chevelle and their immediate retreat would have made pursuit a waste of time if Vern hadn't been driving a powerful vehicle built specifically for high-speed pursuit. It was a 440 Dodge Magnum and the high-speed chase that followed tested both the vehicles and the drivers. Both cars were going too fast as they attempted to make a high speed turn onto

21st Street, so they both spun out. Thinking that he'd end the episode right there by preventing any further attempt to escape, Vern jumped out of his car and from a range of less than five feet he fired six shots into the left rear tire of the Chevelle with his service .38. What he didn't know until his gun was empty was that the tires on the Chevelle were self-sealing which meant that they were virtually puncture proof, so the Chevelle was still in the race while Vern had to scramble back to his car to try to catch up. This time, both cars were heading west very fast on 21st Street and the Chevy had enough of a lead that it beat a slow-moving switch engine through the rail crossing at the stockyards. Vern was far enough behind that he had to stand on the brakes and at that speed, the action turned the hot Dodge sideways. Vern remembers that his friend Tippet was repeating the Rosary over and over while Canfield kept yelling **"Dammit Vern! You're gonna kill us all!"** Vern doesn't know how fast they were going when he hit the brakes, but he says it seemed like they slid for a mile with his heart in his throat and Canfield was screaming all the way. The panic stop allowed the big switch engine to get through the intersection before the police car slid sideways across the tracks right behind the big diesel. By the time Vern had recovered control of the Dodge, the Chevy was out of sight.

The birdshot was plucked out of the four victims (including Vern) at the hospital and the police patiently went to work to find that hot Chevy. Now if they'd wanted to make Vern mad, birdshot was certainly a good choice 'cause he was really steaming! Since the perpetrator's car was so unusual, it didn't take long for all the police in the County to canvass the new car dealers to try to find it, but the most serious lead came from a lady who'd seen news of the chase on television. She called to report that a car matching the description had pulled into a garage across the street and that its occupants had pulled the door closed without turning on the lights in the garage. The police checked it out, found that the car had left without being noticed, but now they knew who the owner of the car was and where he worked from the dealer who'd sold it. Sure enough, they found the car sitting in a Boeing parking lot the next day, got a search warrant to open the trunk and there was the tire with the six bullet penetrations. The owner was arrested later that day as he approached the car at shift change and he confessed that he had been the driver. He gave up the shooter who in turn gave up the other two. Admitting that it was a racially motivated prank intended to scare the blacks, the participants were tried separately for having conspired to commit a crime, but a conspiracy was not proven so only the driver and the shooter were convicted for their respective crimes.

Wichita Eagle Sept. 5, 7, 15, 16, 1967

Maintaining the peace and protecting the public is the primary job of all policemen and sometimes the offenders are the very people we hire to conduct business for us. One such case involved, a County Commissioner who was accused of accepting gifts and cash from firms that provided services and supplies to the County, then lying to a County court during an investigation of County purchasing practices. The State Supreme Court removed the Commissioner from his position and he was sent to prison, escorted by Vern. It was one of the saddest such escorts he'd had to perform because Vern had once served as a lieutenant under the Commissioner when he had been a Captain under Sheriff Ty Lockett.

There is no best place or right time to discuss the part of their job that all policemen dread, but this page is where the subject of the notification of next of kin has landed. Death from natural causes, accidents and automobile crashes that are a daily fact of life ranging from the most minor fender benders in parking lots to huge pileups and conflagrations on our highways, too many of which result in fatalities and the occasional homicide provide us with a national average of one death every several minutes. The severely traumatic and frequently life-threatening injuries at the scenes of those traffic accidents and incidents are handled as efficiently as possible to prevent further damage to human flesh and psyches while the fatalities are removed from public view as quickly and discreetly as possible to prevent further emotional trauma. Over 45,000 people die on our streets and highways every year, almost guaranteeing that sooner or later every police officer will be faced with telling a family member that their loved one is no longer among us.

Being the bearer of such news takes an emotional toll on the messenger and many police officers nowadays require periodic counseling because of it. One of the difficult parts of the aftermath of a fatal crash is that the highest-ranking officer at the scene is obligated to either perform or delegate the notification of the next of kin. For most of us, the unexpected appearance of a police officer at our door in itself is an unusual, unsettling event that instantly creates a severe sense of foreboding that something's gone horribly wrong. Law officers understand that such an appearance immediately conjures the image of a messenger of bad news, but understanding doesn't make the task easier. Even as the highest ranking police officer in Sedgwick County, Vern would frequently appear at the scene of accidents, adding his help by directing traffic, helping collect accident reports ...and notifying the next of kin and close friends of the violent death of a loved one. When the subject is mentioned today, he shakes his head sadly and he gets quiet for awhile, obviously remembering some of those cases. He rarely ever delegated this responsibility.

Sports Car Races, Lake Garnett, Kansas 1969

Moving on to a much happier subject, the annual sports car races at Lake Garnett had become increasingly more difficult for the local police to handle. The last year's enthusiasts had become so rowdy that major crowd disturbances had threatened to overwhelm the police, causing Sheriff Bill Gadelman of Anderson County to request mutual aid from the Sedgwick County sheriff in order to head off a full-blown riot at the next year's races. Since Vern's force was the largest in the state and he was recognized as the most aggressive, most experienced sheriff in the state at the time he was requested to orchestrate the crowd control. He had almost a full year to analyze the situation and he'd had some serious experiences with crowd control, so rather than opt for the pure and simple force of riot police, he chose to employ a slightly more complex tactic called imagery and distraction. Yes, it's actually "smoke and mirrors without cameras". It worked like a charm, causing several witnesses to the event to remark that they'd never seen so many pleasant policemen in one place.

There were about 40 officers on foot that were directing traffic and parking (one even grinned broadly and jigged a few steps to amuse the incoming party-goers). The officers changed locations frequently in order to give the appearance of there being lots more of them than there actually were. But the real showcase part of the force was 22 of the shiny motorcycle brigade riding slowly in formation, the throbbing sound of their powerful engines overwhelming the ears of the crowd as they toured the town and the race grounds over and over. It brought lots of comments, provided grist for lots of conversation and even elicited some good-natured hooting and heckling, but all of the Officers had strict orders to smile a lot and wave to elicit good rapport with the crowd. All in all, the plan worked like a charm. Vern had told his officers "Keep 'em in a good mood and they'll behave!" and he followed that with "It's a whole lot easier to talk somebody out of a bad mood than it is to get the cuffs on them". That sounds like a bit like some cowboy/plowboy philosophy from Marshal Dillon on the old TV show "Gunsmoke" and Paladin in "Have Gun, Will Travel", doesn't it? Well, it worked just fine and a good time was had by all. In addition, it became a textbook study in crowd control for law officers in the years to follow.

Most of the motorcycle brigade were Sheriff's Reserve Officers, a group of men who were intensely loyal to the charismatic Miller. One of those Reserves was the very likeable Bernie Ward, a news reporter for the Wichita Eagle-Beacon and personal friend to Vern. Bernie's dead now, but among some of his notes I found several comments that he'd been was amazed at how well Vern had read that crowd. He'd anticipated their moves many months in advance and conducted the planning of the security force to keep the energy of the crowd of many thousands channeled, their personal safety as well as their mood well under control.

Sheriff Vern Miller, second from left, led motorcycle unit into Lake Garnett race

porter Behind Badge Sees
Edge of Violence Averted

Bernie Ward.

Before we move along to get back to Vern's saga, I'd like to point out that Bernie Ward actually started to write Vern's memoirs entitled "...With Both Feet" and frankly, I consider it an honor to quote him in places in order to finish what Bernie started.

Wichita Beacon, May 6, 1969
Landmark Case
State of Kansas v. Thomas Undorf & Sonya Salas

Just what constitutes a legal search and seizure had already long been an area of intense debate and some small parts of it are still in dispute even today. One tiny but significant piece of that legality was answered by the Kansas State Supreme Court in July of 1972. It sprang from the appeal of a case that began in May of 1969 when a man named Thomas Undorf and his girlfriend/ accomplice, Sonya Salas were caught, arrested and tried in Sedgwick County for the burglary of a Lincoln County drugstore and attempting to sell the stolen controlled substances.

What happened was that Detective Syd Werbin got a tip that someone was offering large quantities of some prescription drugs for sale in the Waterhole Club, one of the night clubs in the north end of Wichita, so Sid and Vern started in that direction. As they approached the club a 1969 Mustang came roaring out of the driveway with wheels spinning, so they turned around and followed. After observing the car being operated erratically, they executed the traffic stop. One of the first things they saw inside the car were drinking glasses with what appeared to be alcoholic drinks in them and there was an open bottle on the console, so the man and woman were ordered out of the car and searched. Then the lawmen noticed a cardboard box containing several un-opened bottles of expensive whiskey on the back seat and Undorf claimed that he'd bought the liquor from "some guy" whose name he couldn't remember "up the street". That's a definite no-no on a Sunday in a Blue Law state and it led Vern to ask if there was anything illegal in the trunk. Undorf, shrugged and disclaimed knowledge of the contents of the trunk and then revealed that the car was leased and didn't belong to him. Since the legal owner of the car wasn't present the officers assumed that they were free to search the trunk and its contents without a search warrant and that's where the stolen narcotics were found with the fingerprints of the pair in custody all over them.

As the foursome prepared to make the short trip downtown to jail, Vern and Syd noticed that Salas was digging around in her purse. Simultaneously, they realized that the purse hadn't been searched, so there was a brief scramble to get it away from her and sure enough, there was a loaded, unlicensed pistol in it. Maybe she had intended to use it or maybe she hadn't even considered it, but she was charged with another count.

Tom Undorf died later while in prison when he was thrown off the third tier of the cell block at Lansing Penitentiary.

U.S. Federal Court file, Osmond Herbert Jr. and Larry Allen Egan W-CR-1237 filed 6/22/70
Master Detective Magazine, October 1970

In April of 1970, Vern was involved in an incident that had the potential for a major disaster if he had failed to act quickly and decisively. National Guard armories in Harper and Medicine Lodge had been burglarized and the list of missing weapons included a large number of the easily sold .45 caliber semi-automatic pistol, an M60 fully automatic rifle (machine gun), a recoilless rifle capable of penetrating armor plate and plenty of ammunition for all of the weapons. It was easy to deduce that the pistols would be sold on the street for instant cash, but the sole purpose of the 30 calibre M60 is to take on large numbers of opponents or at least keep them pinned down with 550 shots per minute. It's not a large piece of machinery, but it's an extremely serious, death-dealing weapon of war that's been known to cut a man in half in combat. The recoilless rifle, on the other hand, is about the size of a large shotgun and it could conceivably be used to either penetrate some types of bank safes, cripple and open an armored truck like a can opener or stop small armored vehicles used by police in standoff situations. It's not hard to imagine what it would do to the standard police car and its occupants. That was quite a truckload of deadly weapons! The order went out at all levels of law enforcement to find and secure those weapons immediately!

With that many eyes and ears on full-alert, it didn't take long for the Sheriff's sources to come up with the names and location of the thieves. Immediately, Vern notified Elmer Fletcher, agent in charge of the local FBI office requesting instructions. Agent Fletcher instructed Miller to proceed with the case and "......Get those guns back!" Vern quietly deployed his officers around the house as soon as it got dark and the lawmen shivered while they waited the many long hours , straining to see through the darkness. The relative humidity was very high, so the tall grass they were lying in was soon drenched in dew, adding to their cold, miserable discomfort. They waited through the long hours, then suddenly, two men came out of the house and got in the car that was parked in the driveway. The officers knew all too well the value of the element of surprise, so they sprung the ambush when their adversaries were most vulnerable. The engine started and the two were just about to back out of the driveway when the Vern ran to the driver's side and jerked the door open with his pistol pointed at the driver's face. The driver reacted in panic and hit the brakes while grabbing one of the two loaded .45s on the seat just as he was dragged out and the gun swung around to point right at Vern's head. Miller saw it coming and dropped to the ground as he swung his own legs to take the man's legs out from under him. The pistol went skidding harmlessly across the grass and from there it was just another wrestling match to get the handcuffs on. The other guy made an effort to point his gun at Vern too, but he surrendered when he realized that there were a lot of guns pointing at his ear from very close range.

The bust turned out to be a real jackpot! The driver turned out to be none other than Osmond Herbert Jr. from Chicago, an ex-con who had hacksawed his way out of the Pratt County Jail just two months earlier where he'd been incarcerated for impersonating a Federal law officer and bad check charges. More than two dozen Kansas counties wanted him, so once he was arrested, Mr. Herbert was to go nowhere without shackles for a number of years. Herbert's partner-in-crime, Larry Allen Egan, was pretty much a bird of the same feather except that he was from Wichita. Herbert was tried quickly and sentenced to Lansing with a Federal detainer for the list of felony weapons charges that he would be tried for at a later date. Egan saw that he had no defense, so he threw up his hands and pled guilty to the Federal charges.

Detective Walker and Det. Baker check machine gun recovered after armory theft.

Wichita Beacon June 6, 1969

The roadblock system that Miller had developed several years earlier was tested again late on the night of June 5th when someone robbed a gas station north of Wellington and murdered the attendant. Neighbors heard the shots and witnessed a late model Chevrolet leaving the scene in a hurry and headed north toward Wichita. Wellington police quickly phoned the warning to

Vern and he activated the roadblock, adding backup units along U.S. 81 in case the Chevy got around the roadblock. Sure enough, the suspect resorted to using country roads and it was one of the backup units that spotted the Chevy when it returned to the main highway just south of Wichita. Deputy John Dotson was the first to see the car as it went through Haysville headed north. Dotson had only been on full-time duty for two months, but he knew that this was not a guy to approach alone. He called for backup and waited for the other officers to get in position before he ordered the car to stop. Donald Sweat offered no resistance. He was arrested and booked into the Sedgwick County Jail where the Sumner County Sheriff picked him up to transport Sweat and his 11-year-old son back to Wellington. The young boy had been in the car all along.

Even back in those days when instant communications didn't exist yet between law enforcement agencies, it didn't take long to discover that the Chevy had been stolen earlier that day from Quality Chevrolet in Wichita, so grand theft auto was added to the first degree murder charge.

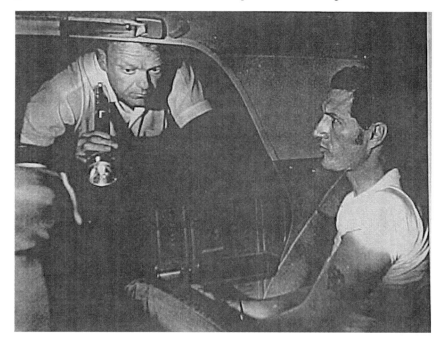

Donald Sweat didn't have much to say to Sheriff Miller.

Search and Rescue

Finding and helping people in accidental trouble has long been the responsibility of law enforcement. Rescuing those people from life-threatening situations was frequently a real problem because few departments had the training or equipment suitable for such undertakings. The movement to develop such services had to start somewhere and police departments were the most visible in those days, so they got the initial call. Many police departments struggled with this and some attained some level of success although the responsibility for most Search and Rescue efforts nationwide made a quick swing to fire departments in the early seventies. However, early in his tenure as Sheriff it became evident to Vern that his officers were being utilized more and more to rescue citizens in trouble, so he set out to get his deputies trained and equipped to meet all emergencies. After auto crashes, the water-borne accidents and industrial tragedies seemed to be the most frequent life-and-death problems faced, so he went to work making sure that his officers could swim, got some of them, including himself, certified in underwater retrieval and finally began acquiring very mobil boats of various types. The largest of his fleet was a U.S. Navy DUKW that had been donated to the County by the Wichita Eagle-Beacon. It was an amphibious truck/boat that was large and awkward on land where it propelled itself, but once in the water it made a great platform for his divers to work from because it was so stable. It could remain on station almost indefinitely and best of all, it could launch itself almost anywhere just by driving into the water. This picture shows it out on the road with a typical escort.

The next picture shows Sheriff Miller and the Rescue Crew on the deck of "Huckleberry Duck" under way as they prepare to send a diver down.

MILLER'S LAW

It's ironic that Vern has gained nearly as much notoriety in his lifetime by challenging laws and law enforcement as he has in enforcing our laws. One such example put him in a potentially dangerous confrontation with three other lawmen. This is how it came about.

Wichita Eagle Oct. 3, 4, & 5, 1967

One story frequently leads into another and this one follows that pattern. He was sitting in his office minding his sheriff-business one day when his phone rang. It was the mother of a young man who'd once been a member of Vern boxing team and she was upset. It seems that her son had managed to get in trouble with the law, which got him sent to a juvenile detention camp, but he'd elected to walk away from the camp which got him labeled as an escapee with a warrant out for his arrest. Not long after, the youngster had called his mother and she'd managed to talk him into surrendering, but he was only willing to surrender to Vern because of the trust he'd developed for Vern. What made that a little ticklish was that the boy was in Leavenworth County, but the mother begged and pleaded and Vern finally consented to drive to Leavenworth with her to pick up her son. As she'd arranged with her son, they arrived at the railroad station and waited…and waited, but the boy didn't appear, for whatever reason. Vern and the mother finally decided to cruise the bars and taverns in the neighborhood, hoping against hope to find him, but to no avail. However, most of the places they visited had gambling machines of various types operating in plain sight and the lady asked Vern why he didn't arrest the operators, to which he responded that he was outside his legal jurisdiction. He didn't like it either because he knew that what he was seeing was illegal, but he refused to interfere, at least for the time being, and they went back to Wichita empty-handed and disappointed.

Only a few days later, Vern was asked to give his official opinion to a State Legislature's committee on the subject of consolidating city and county police departments into so-called metropolitan police departments. This was a concept that was being proposed in order to improve efficiency of operation and the legislature was merely investigating the idea. Vern didn't think much of the idea and said so, even quoting several examples that could easily cause the project to fail and one of those examples was Leavenworth county which Vern described as being "wide open with slot machines and one-armed bandits all over the place." He was bluntly candid about his recent observations in Leavenworth and remarked that liquor and gambling laws were certainly not winked at in his county. Naturally, his comments hit the news statewide, which was bound to rub somebody the wrong way …and it did.

The Prosecuting Attorney for Leavenworth County was livid! He was so incensed that he decided to set Vern up to have him arrested on trumped up charges in order to discredit him. He initiated an inquisition and subpoenaed Vern into his jurisdiction to testify under oath about what gambling activities he'd seen in Leavenworth County. Now he had based this action on the assumption that Vern would waffle and try to soften his comments, thereby contradicting his sworn testimony to the lawmakers, which of course would constitute perjury and make him liable for arrest, discrediting his testimony forever. A few days later, the Undersheriff from Leavenworth County delivered the subpoena while Vern was directing shift change traffic at Boeing. The UnderSheriff was friendly to Vern, so he told Vern confidentially that the County Attorney intended to put Vern in jail for perjury and that he should bring an attorney with him.

That's when Vern decided to contact Ernest McRae, a former FBI agent who was practicing law in Wichita. He filled Ernie in on the details, then the two of them drove to Leavenworth County to answer the subpoena. After they'd sat in the waiting room for much longer than was polite for an invited guest, the County Attorney walked in saying brusquely "Come in my office and give your statement." When Ernie got up to accompany Vern, the County Attorney stopped him, saying "Not you. Vern will give his statement alone."

Ernie saw the trap being set, so he replied sharply "In light of what we've heard, **when** Sheriff Miller gives his statement, I'll be with him."

The County Attorney was furious with Ernie, tempers flared and the volume went up. While they were arguing the fine points of law at full volume, a District Court judge wearing his judical robe walked by enroute to his office. Vern and Ernie broke off the dispute with the Prosecuting Attorney and followed the judge into his office, telling him about the suspected frame-up. The judge replied "Well, the Sheriff (Vern) has caused a lot of problems with his ill-considered statements".

At that moment, Ernie noticed the judge's nameplate and that his last name was the same as the County Attorney.   That was the last straw to McRea, so he stood up, said "Thanks, Judge" and he and Vern walked back into the waiting room.

The County Attorney asked Vern "Are you coming in?"

Vern replied "Not without my attorney."

That's when the County Attorney turned to two uniformed police officers and ordered them to "Arrest him."

Vern's right hand immediately went to rest on his pistol and his facial expression showed his anger. His resolve was clear, "If either of you move, I'll kill you!" he snapped. The air was thick with the electricity of the tension; it was an eyebal-to-eyeball staredown and Vern was a split-second from deadly action. Ernie told me that those several seconds seemed like an eternity to him. Fortunately for all concerned, surprise, fear, or good judgement froze both Deputies right where they sat and their hands didn't move, so Vern and Ernie quickly backed out of the room and they walked very briskly to where they'd parked their car. As they stepped into their car, a Deputy Sheriff ran to their car and handed Vern another subpoena to appear at another inquisition sometime later.

Vern and Ernie were incensed by the treatment they'd received, so they didn't waste time driving back to Wichita; they drove straight to Attorney General Londerholm's office in Topeka and explained what'd happened. Ernie told the Attorney General that "We'll be returning to honor their subpoena, but we'll be bringing thirty armed Deputies with us to insure that there'll be no more strong arm behavior like that." The irate pair made it clear to Londerholm that Sedgwick County's police were ready to go to war with their neighbor if there was any further antagonism from that quarter.

Vern and Ernie returned to Wichita and as they exited the Kansas Turnpike at Eastgate, the Turnpike attendant handed them a radio gram from Leavenworth which stated "Inquisition subpoena cancelled. Do not return to Leavenworth." The tension had been broken, but they kept a watchful eye on that political sector from then on. Vern speculates that the Attorney General had quickly intervened to head off further confrontation on any level.

There was extensive news media coverage because the Leavenworth County Prosecutor had arranged for Vern's arrest to be well-covered. This apparently devious behavior of one of the combatants combined with the hot-headed reaction of the other made such a splash in the news that the State Legislature simply couldn't ignore it, so in the very next session the legislators passed a law that we still live by today. What is known in Kansas simply as "Miller's Law" makes it unlawful to resist arrest by any law officer, even if the arrest itself is clearly and obviously unlawful.

After he'd related the event, Vern said thoughtfully that "It was not my proudest moment, but I did it knowing full well what the consequences could be regardless how it (the confrontation) turned out."

His answer to the next question was already obvious, but had to be asked. "So what would you have done if those two deputies had made a threatening move?"

He was already shaking his head slowly and sadly as he said without hesitation "It would've turned out badly…very, very badly. At that moment I had already made up my mind that nobody was going to put me in jail for telling the truth regardless what I had to do to stop him or them. "

I interviewed Ernie sometime later and one of his comments was that it had been one of the most extremely tense situations of his entire life. "I could feel those bullets in my back as we walked briskly to the car and I was real glad to see that message telling us that the subpoena had been cancelled."

Salute From A Rolling Harley

Beech Aircraft August 5, 1969
Reprinted, Wichita Eagle 12/23/2007

The end of the labor strike against Beech Aircraft had just been annouced and the crowd on the sidewalk outside the Beech factory was cheering the conclusion. Adding his own flavor to the celebration, the very popular Sheriff mounted a standard-issue Harley Davidson patrol bike (it appears to be an Electra) and executed a circus trick known as a'stand-up ride-by' to salute the crowd of mechanics to thank them for having conducted a long strike peacefully.

For those interested in the details of how he did it, Vern says that the Electra was very stable at speeds above 30 mph with the throttle locked and he thinks he locked it at 41-45 mph for this pass. The cheering of the crowd swelled to a roar as he passed and a non-striking Beech employee in the administration building shot this photograph over the heads of the waving, cheering crowd with a long range telephoto lens.

8-5-69   35054-2819 BEECH AIRCRAFT CORP.

Wichita Eagle-Beacon Feb. 17, 18, 19 & Mar. 2, 1969
Inside Detective Magazine June 1969

Ken Ketter was 20 when he died of a severe blow to the back of his head, or stab wounds or a gunshot. It was cold and the snow was deeper than usual in south central Kansas. His roommate found a lot of blood, signs of a struggle and spilled groceries in the driveway one evening but no sign of Ken, so he called police. A forensic appraisal of the scene determined that quite a struggle had happened approximately 15 hours earlier, so the search for Ken Ketter began.

Several days and lots of questioning later, a tip sent Vern leading a convoy of police cars loaded with officers dressed for bad weather to search a shallow strip of the Ninnescah River east of Viola, Kansas. They found Ken Ketter's body in shallow water clad only in his underwear.

Sheriff's truck bogged down in snow bringing out victim's brutalized body.

The intense investigation that followed revealed that Ketter had an enemy with a motive to kill him over a woman. That man had shared a room with Ketter briefly almost a year earlier. He was Chester Mefford who was separated from his attractive, blond wife. It seems that bad blood had formed between Ketter and Mefford when Mefford's wife had appeared at the apartment, got into a violent argument with Mefford and he'd beaten her. He had a record of domestic violence and several other physical confrontations, so this wasn't Mefford's first display of violence. Ketter had intervened as Mefford was beating her and Mefford left in a rage.

After the encounter, the woman had asked Ketter to drive her home, Mefford soon got wind of it and that's where the deadly trouble started. Some time later, Mefford waylayed Ketter, they got into a scuffle and Mefford pulled a knife, but Ketter somehow managed to disarm him and filed a complaint with the Wichita Police.

That was the end of it for awhile. Mefford found another place to live, but he didn't forget and it worked on him. Time didn't heal his wounded ego, whether there was basis for it or not. His jealousy had consumed him, so finally he arranged to get revenge. Almost a year later, he enlisted the aid of three of his friends and ambushed Ketter in the driveway as Ken arrived home with his groceries.

According to Ralph Cluck's testimony during the trial, he was driving on the night of the assault, so he stayed in the car with the engine running while Mefford, Robert Campbell and an unnamed teenager hid behind Ketter's apartment. When Ketter arrived, the ambush was sprung. One of them cracked him on the back of his head as he got his groceries out of his car, then the three of them beat him until he fell unconscious and quit resisting.

They loaded him in the back seat of Cluck's car and drove southwest on K-42 toward Viola. When they reached the Ninnescah River, they turned off the highway onto a county road. It was dark, the snow was deep and the ground was frozen hard, so they dragged him to the riverbank. It was here that Mefford uttered the words that surprised Cluck since he thought Ketter was already dead. "This is as good a place as any to do him in." Mefford jumped astraddle of Ketter with a knife in hand and when he raised the weapon, Ketter raised a hand to deflect the deadly blow. That's when Campbell pulled the trigger of the pistol he'd been holding just inches from the side of Ketter's head. As the gun went off, Mefford brought the knife down repeatedly, even stabbing Ketter in the heart once again after they'd removed his clothes. Then they threw him in the Ninnescah River, gathered up his clothes and tossed them in the Arkansas River, miles from the scene of the murder.

Three days into selection of the jury, Chester Mefford changed his plea to guilty and was subsequently sentenced to two life terms for the kidnapping and murder of Ken Ketter. Two weeks later, he made two different attempts to kill himself with razor blades that had been slipped to him by other prisoners who didn't like him. On the second of those suicide attempts, Vern was called from his office and he succeeded in taking the razor away from Mefford.

Wichita Beacon April 16, 1969

The evening of April 13th of 1969, Mulvane farmer Ward Statts, Jr. was sitting in his easy chair reading when he heard two shots outside and since it was well after dark, he knew that it couldn't be a hunter so he went to a window to investigate. He saw a car parked several hundred yards down the road from his farm and as he peered through the dim light, he saw a figure get out of the car and appeared to put something fairly large in the trunk, then got back in the car and drove away. It was unusual behavior and it bothered Statts, so he mentioned the incident to a friend the next day; his friend advised him to report it to the police, the sooner the better. The report went through the Derby Police who quickly determined that a potential homicide was too big for them to handle, so it landed on Vern's phone. He listened patiently, then arranged to meet Statts to look at the site. A few hours later, they were standing looking down at two small splashes of blood when Vern saw something that seemed oddly out of place, so he picked up what looked like part of a tooth. He took the tooth fragment and a small sample of blood to someone he knew at Wichita State University who confirmed that both samples were from a human. The testimony of the witness combined with the evidence was enough to launch a murder investigation and that always gets the attention of the press.

Ironically, it was the press coverage that caused an eyewitness to the event to worry enough about his own involvement to consult an attorney who in turn called Vern to arrange a meeting. The young man had quite a story to tell and it began at a club called the Red Slipper. On the night in question, he'd been drinking with an off-duty bartender named Randy Hill whose wife also worked at the club. For some reason, Hill was convinced that another man, Robert Koon a.k.a. Bob Evans, had been sleeping with Hill's wife. When Hill confronted Koon/Evans with his suspicion, naturally Koon had denied it. Hill didn't believe him and had shoved a gun in Koon's ribs while they were still inside the club, telling him quietly to go outside where they could talk in private and apparently no one else saw them leave. The three of them had gotten in Hill's car and driven to a secluded spot near Mulvane where Hill shot Koon three times. The witness claimed that he'd been stunned and terrified, but it was far from over. Hill insisted that the witness help load the body in the trunk and that he drive to northern Kansas where they hid the body under an empty stock tank, then they returned to Wichita.

The Sheriff listened to the story intently, then ordered a small search team assembled while he called the Sheriff of the northern Kansas County and the entourage drove north. The weather was miserable all the way, especially when they arrived. It was drizzling rain and there was a late spring snow on the ground at their destination. Even traveling around on the muddy country roads around the farm community near Wilson, Kansas was difficult, but the local Sheriff knew his territory well and he led the small party to wherever they needed to go. The witness wasn't able to identify exactly where the stock tank was, so after searching a number of potential sites, a group of three of the local farmers had put their heads together and come up with a site they thought fit the vague description and the investigative team went to check it out. They found the stock tank, there was a corpse underneath it and an arrest warrant was immediately issued for Randy Hill. He was picked up in south Wichita, charged with first-degree kidnapping, first-degree murder, felonious assault and robbery and he was convicted on all counts.

On December 18th of 1969, Randall C. Hill was sentenced to two consecutive life sentences.

Upward and Onward With 'True Grit'

Although it has some questionable merit, the Predestination Theory (a great Master Plan laid out in finite detail) could explain why lots of things happen. Following this assumption, it was simply time for Vern to move onward and upward from the Sheriff's desk he'd occupied for six years. One day in 1969, Democratic Governor Bob Docking made a special trip to Wichita to talk to Vern, specifically to ask him to run for the position of Attorney General in the upcoming election. Docking admitted readily that the odds were that Vern probably lose, that "This is primarily a Republican state and there has never been a Democrat elected to Attorney General here." However, Docking's reasoning was "With your name recognition and image, whether you win or lose, it'll distract the voters from my race with Kent Frizzell for the Governor's office. In addition, your name on the ballot will bring out the Democratic voters in huge numbers." Docking was referring to the large numbers of voters who turned out each time Vern's name appeared on the ballot.

Wichita Beacon June 17, 1970
Wichita Eagle June 18, 1970

Ever since Vern had attained his law degree and been admitted to the bar, he'd wanted to practice law. This wasn't his preferred course of action, but he felt that running for Attorney General would be a graceful way to leave the Sheriff's Office that he'd occupied for a record three terms already. The flip side was that his wife Ella Mae was adamantly opposed to politics in any form and had filed for divorce on June 8, right after he'd told her that he would run for the office of Attorney General.

It'd be real easy for events to get out of sequence again since so much happened all at once, so we'll start by looking at a potentially disastrous event in his career that was immediately labeled with facetious humorous as

92

"True Grit!" by the press. Soon after announcing his candidacy for Attorney General, Vern was headed for the annual Kansas State Fair in Hutchinson to deliver a campaign speech. He was dressed in his best Sunday suit and driving an unmarked car when he heard a call on the radio for assistance to quell a disturbance at Heights High School where the student body was primarily black. Realizing that this was a racial hotspot that could easily turn into a full-blown race riot, he quickly turned his car around and raced back to the scene.

The Sheriff was one of the first officers arriving on the scene and the first thing he saw when he ran inside the high school were several young blacks beating and kicking a young white female student who'd been knocked to the floor. He rushed to her defense and immediately found himself being mobbed by a group of black teenagers as they tried to get him on the ground so they could dogpile him (hold him down so they could beat and kick him), but that tactic didn't work very well. The pugnacious Sheriff went down three or four different times, but each time he struggled free and bounced up, slamming his knuckles into any head that came in range and quite a few of those who got hit stayed on the ground for the duration. It was a first-class donnybrook and the rowdy teenagers were getting a valuable lesson from a well-trained old pro who was good at what they'd provoked.

The limited-action brawl lasted for over an hour even after the Deputies, Wichita Police and State Troopers began arriving to quell the small racial war and the novices quickly discovered that they were no match for the hand-picked, well-trained, seasoned veterans with their Mace and nightsticks. At the peak of the battle the air was thick with angry yells, snarled epithets and the burning stink of Mace. The sounds of riot battle are a confused cacaphony; I've been there so I can tell you from experience that nightsticks make a "thunk" when they connect with a human head, flashlights make a distinctive "tonk" sound while fists make a sound that's much more like a "splat". The combat zone got so crowded that at one point some of the officers discarded their nightsticks and flashlights since there wasn't enough room to swing them. It was a huge wrestling/punching/snarling dog pile. When it was finally over, several officers went to the hospital for bumps, bruises, strains and scrapes suffered in the brawl, but a much larger number of students were treated, mostly for some serious headaches, split lips and eyebrows, broken noses and numerous abrasions. Over two dozen rioters were handcuffed and hauled off to jail while those who weren't arrested made their own way to medical help. The Sheriff and his good suit were a little worse for the wear too and he was certainly battle weary, but otherwise he was pretty much intact. Vern wasn't at all pleased that the law officers had been forced to resort to violence to restore the peace, but he was greatly relieved that no serious injuries were reported. When he was examined later in the Emergency Room it was discovered that he had numerous cuts, bruises, scrapes and a gorgeous black eye that a press photographer gleefully committed to history. Oh yes, everybody who'd been involved either had torn clothing or was blood-spattered, including Vern.

Hutchinson News Feb. 26, 1971
Wichita Beacon Feb. 26, 1971 June 21 & 22, 1971

Somehow, the Hutchinson newspaper scooped all the other newspapers and ran a front-page story of the fracas featuring a large photo of Vern prominently sporting his black eye. Not only that, they entitled the accompanying article "True Grit Brought To Kansas Politics." Parts of it ran in subsequent issues of all the other papers and especially that photo. It ran in most of the newspapers in the state and the laughable rumor that quickly made the rounds was that the owners of the Hutchinson News, who were openly staunch Republicans, had threatened to fire the reporter for giving a Democrat such great publicity. The rumor was probably untrue, but of all the news articles written about Vern during this campaign, the words "True Grit" were certainly the most influential on the voters when they went to the polls a month later. Vern had established yet another first, it was that no other candidate for Attorney General had ever run for the office while sporting a black eye that he got for defending a future constituent. Political wags, pundits and cartoonists milked that one for all it was worth for years afterward.

MILLER'S FAIR poster doesn't show the shiner.

True Grit Brought
To Kansas Politics

I apologize for the poor quality of the photo; it was the very best that I could find, but you can see that the owner had really taken a hard whack and he wasn't the least bit ashamed of his battle scar.

Campaign promises are what 1) get political aspirants elected, 2) get them in trouble or 3) both ...and for Vern, it was both. Early in the campaign, one of Vern's promises had the distinct look of such a make-or-break statement. He'd sworn to his audience that if he were elected "..I'll land in the middle of the drug-ridden hippie commune at Lawrence with both feet!" He'd read the voting, tax-paying public perfectly and with the timely publicity provided by the "True Grit" article, the gamble paid off.

Given his long track record and his credentials combined with his newly freshened popularity with the voters because of "True Grit", he had the full support of the Democratic Party. Vern ran his typically aggressive and extremely energetic campaign that resulted in his election, winning by a healthy margin. He'd enjoyed the campaign battle, but the folks on his campaign staff were totally exhausted when it was over. It was a stunning, overwhelming victory that for the first time in almost a century matched a Democratic Governor with a Democratic Attorney General. The office was an awesome responsibility, but he wasn't intimidated and he proudly became the first County Sheriff in the United States to be elected Attorney General of his state.

Attorney General of the State of Kansas

Once again, the famous black-or-white, right-or-wrong intellect for which he'd become famous kicked in. He quickly reviewed the pending cases and files left behind by his predecessor and distributed the assignments among his enthusiastic staff. Almost as if to amuse historians three decades later, several things immediately happened all at the same time. The first was a press conference during which Vern declared bluntly that "Drugs are Public Enemy No. 1!" and he followed that with urging for equal enforcement of our laws, setting the stage for delivering on his campaign promise. Right on its heels, the exuberant press encouraged their clear favorite by dragging out that photo labeled "True Grit" to run it again and again with the article. The timing for that photo was nearly perfect; it sure got the public's attention again and the article about the riot mentioned that his bill from the Emergency Room was $42 plus some odd cents. Oddly though, it didn't mention the cost of treating the injuries of the other officers, the teenagers or even the cost of replacing his business suit.

As happens to most elected dignitaries, he was immediately the darling of the guest speaker circuit in his new capacity, this time as gladiator-turned-statesman. For the first one, he was still wearing the remnants of a dandy shiner and the crowd knew where he'd gotten it. "Yeah", he said somewhat sheepishly, sounding as much like his favorite comedian Bob Hope as he could, "A funny thing happened to me on the way to Hutchinson a while back.....". The audience already knew what'd happened; the news media had been full of it for several days, but they just wanted to hear him tell it in his own words. Anyway, after the show-stopping laughter finally subsided he went on to talk about the incident where he wound up on the bottom of a dog pile of flailing teenagers. The guy who told me the story couldn't remember what the rest of Vern's speech had been about, but he remembered Vern's opening statement vividly.

This incident seems almost insignificant in comparison to the rest of this story, but Paula Miller delighted in telling it to me over dinner one evening and I saw its value immediately. She'd been a secretary for the State assigned to the Attorney General's office staff for some time before Vern arrived to take office. As he walked into his office area on one of his first days in office he noticed a small crowd of his office staff collected around the door to one of the office cubicles. This behavior seemed unusual and it attracted his attention, so he walked over to investigate. It turned out that the A.G. Deputy Attorney who occupied the office cubicle had misplaced his key to the cubicle and the small crowd was waiting for someone from the building maintenance department to arrive with a master key to unlock the door. Vern wasn't fazed for even an instant. He went over that wall like a nimble teenager vaulting a backyard fence and within seconds he opened the door from the inside. He'd used that maneuver and others like it numerous times in foot pursuits over the years in law enforcement, so it was a well-practiced move. His newly-acquired staff was amazed because their previous bosses had always been desk-bound attorneys while Vern was a law enforcement officer who'd always worn a badge and a gun, so he was a man of action to suit the situation. It didn't take long for his staff to realize that his simple solution to a simple problem had just raised the bar and that his expectations of them had been elevated dramatically. Their admiration for his decisive action was soon reflected in their performance levels and they immediately went to work to meet the expectations of their new boss. That was also the first time the future Mrs. Miller had seen the muscular Attorney General swing into action and it made a lasting impression. Simple as it was, they all realized as they stood there gaping in awe that this was a man who would not be denied a solution to a problem.

Shortly after taking office, the new Attorney General issued a one-page letter that made his stand on the enforcement of our laws unmistakably clear to Kansas Sheriffs, Police Chiefs and Prosecuting Attorneys. In it he said, "Nothing breeds disrespect for the law more than a double standard in its enforcement". He was referring to illegal drug activities, unlawful gambling (including bingo) illegal liquor violations and selectively "looking the other way". In this same letter he asked that all of the recipients notify all clubs, fraternal and religious organizations alike that "From this time forward, all the laws will be enforced equally and if you have trouble enforcing them, this office is here to help you."

Based on Vern's reputation, there was absolutely no misunderstanding his message, so most law officers and county attorneys agreed and complied with Miller's request, whether they liked it or not. But in every crowd there's always a few who will drag their feet and there were those who did not shut down illegal gambling and liquor dealings immediately, perhaps thinking that he wouldn't follow through. Vern's a "Take charge and git 'er done" guy, so those few procrastinators soon found the Attorney General and his officers in their midst in a series of lightning-like raids, confiscating gambling equipment and filing criminal charges for allowing gambling. The raids were led by the A.G. himself and were conducted in many communities across the state. The largest such raid by police officers that has ever been conducted in Kansas took place in Great Bend on October 2nd and 3rd of 1971.

Meantime, Vern's entire staff was busy playing catch up with the cases his predecessor had bequeathed him while Vern was planning to deliver on his campaign promise to come down hard on crime in Kansas, especially the illegal drug industry. He knew that drugs had quickly become the root cause of most of the crimes committed in the state and that it was time to kick his anti-crime/anti-drug program into overdrive. He was finally the top cop in the state, so now he had the authority, the know-how and the enthusiastic cooperation of police departments and prosecutors statewide, the taxpayer mandate plus a campaign promise that he meant to keep, to "..Land in the hippy community with both feet". Towns, cities and rural communities across the entire state had felt the effects of the pernicious illegal drug business as usage had spread into their jurisdictions. They all wanted to be part of stopping the devastating horror of this deadly social cancer. He'd put the fire back in the eyes of lawmen all over his state.

Within weeks after winning the election, drug raids originating in his office became frequent. They were well-planned, well-coordinated and usually executed simultaneously in numerous cities around the state, sometimes involving as many as 150 officers. Sometimes all of the officers involved in those raids were quietly assembled in the targeted town just before the raid was activated, but none of the participants in the raids were given their target assignment until just minutes before the raids took place and there were no cell phones, so security was tight. The home of the University of Kansas in Lawrence was hit first and most often simply because that's where most of the drug trafficking activity was concentrated. The first raid happened just six weeks after he took office. After that, they frequently hit the same locations and even the same suspects and with as much press and photo coverage as was feasible without jeopardizing the security of the operation. Of course that caused some of the accused to claim harassment which in turn caused Vern to grin and offer the low-key comment that he'd discovered that "The most effective deterrent to crime is a big dose of public attention". The press loved that one and so did the public. Law enforcement in Kansas had never had so much support and so many tips. Very bright lights were being aimed at places where illumination had been unknown and it caused many to scurry for places to hide, mostly out-of-state. As expected, the resident druggies began to race to squeal on each other, either to gain time to run for cover or to worm themselves into the good graces of the Law.

Since no one recorded or remembers how many drug raids Vern instigated as the Attorney General, let's just say that they were numerous and frequent. He kicked off the first operation by leading the team that raided Lawrence and it was a resounding success. Overall, there were more than 150 officers involved that night. They netted 33 suspected users, a large quantity of pot and some of the mind-bending LSD. Some time later, there were raids in as many as 5 cities simultaneously inside the state in the same nights and not all of them were considered successful, but the pattern had been set. That first night had been just for starters and he kept the pressure on by either leading, planning or ordering raids all over the state. It happened again and again, making it obvious that there was definitely a random-repeating cycle, sometimes only days or weeks apart, sometimes several months and it continued year after year while he was in office. It became readily apparent that the most predictable element was that the raids were going to continue as often as there were viable targets. Best of all, it set the example for all law enforcement agencies and they began to stage their own raids.

Some people have the ability to focus tightly on their job or profession and it becomes their life, their reason for waking up each day, their driving force, their reason for living and breathing. Vern has always been extremely focussed even as far back as high school when he wanted to become a professional boxer. During his childhood and teenaged years he'd worked hard for a dairy farm from 4 am until 7 pm every day that he wasn't in school, so he'd developed quite a muscular physique, very well-suited for any physical undertaking he chose. His military service had honed and refined his pile of muscles and added to his ability to focus intently. Twenty-five years later he was well into into his law career, he was at the top of the law enforcement pyramid in the State. Although it was subtle, another of his character traits had surfaced; Vern was frugal. He discovered that he had no desire to drive big shiny cars, live in a big, showy house or wear expensive suits. Fords and Chevys were his choice for transportation and Sears provided his suits. Once into the major political eye of the public as the Attorney General, he had to be prompted to buy tailored business suits and more than one of his political peers was amazed to find that he was frugal almost to a fault when he mentioned that he lived in a mobil home. "Well, it's got everything I need and it's cheap, so I'm happy with it" was his explanation. It didn't endear him to our socially elite, but when news of it got out it quickly made him the absolute darling of the voters of the huge working classes. I sincerely believe that if he'd filed for the Presidency of the United States at that point, he would have carried the State of Kansas.

Wichita Eagle (AP) May 15, 1972

Alf Landon was a highly respected Kansas politician who, at the peak of his career had been Governor of the state and had even been a viable Republican candidate for the Presidency of the United States. The elderly Landon re-appeared on the political scene many years later as the voice of reason during the anti-war demonstrations of the late 60's and early 70's. It happened when Vern stepped in to personally direct local police on the front lines to disperse a large crowd of protesters in the streets of Lawrence, Kansas. This drew the ire of Chancellor Laurence Chalmers of the University of Kansas. Assuming that he was on firm ground because of the politically liberal students with whom he was rather popular, he criticized Vern roundly in the press for applying excessive force in maintaining the peace. Chalmers claimed that Vern's action had been purely for political gain. Aha! Two big-name political heavyweights going head-to-head; the press **loved it!** In retrospect, it couldn't have played out better if the event had been planned to deliberately elicit Vern's characteristic response, knowing full well that he'd take whatever action necessary to protect the peaceful citzenry from the rowdy students who were, for the most part, not yet old enough to vote.

Immediately and without warning or solicitation, the venerable and very respectable Republican Alf Landon rocked the news world by publicly stating his support of the Attorney General's action. The elder statesman made his opinion very clear in the interview as he declared that "Chancellor Chalmers joins chicken fighters, operators of one-armed bandits, private clubs that have gambling and drug peddlers in accusing the Kansas Attorney General, in effect, of playing politics." The notoriously candid Mr. Landon didn't stop there, either. In his typically out-spoken manner, he went on to say that "I cast my first vote in Kansas in 1908. I've never voted for a Democrat Attorney General in all those years. If the Chancellor is right that the Attorney General is playing politics, he's playing the politics I like. As far as I'm concerned, I'm going to vote for the first Democrat Attorney General in all those years. His name is Vern Miller."

It was a stunning slap in the face for the publicly disobedient war protest movement and of course for the Chancellor and yes, Vern was re-elected by a landslide. It seemed that mobs who broke windows, trashed cars and threw Molotov cocktails hadn't pleased the mature voting public, Democrats and Republicans alike.

Then one fine day in 1973, Spice Magazine, a Kansas City periodical known for its very liberal views and philosophies, decided to request an extensive interview with the Attorney General. What they expected was a cool and polite refusal based on his busy schedule from his Public Relations Manager. What they immediately discovered was that he didn't have a PR Manager on his staff or a spin-doctor on call. To their absolute amazement, he didn't even have a telephone receptionist. Their telephone call went straight to Vern's desk and what they got was an immediate acceptance of their request for an interview. Shortly after his acceptance, what they learned from that interview amazed the reporter, the magazine and their readers. Vern was older now and even more bluntly candid and straightforward than he'd been as a uniformed policeman. The reporter certainly hadn't been prepared for that. I've condensed that interview for the sake of brevity. Vern explained to the cynical reporter that the voters had elected him to enforce the laws that we already had on the books without favor to friends or special interests from any direction. Without hesitation, he continued that it was "..Not my job to re-write laws to suit my personal preference, only to enforce them equally and exactly as they were written". The reporter had gone in expecting a torrent of four syllable words, a righteous sermon of legalistic mumbo jumbo, a huge philosophical argument attempting to justify playing the part of an avenging angel like some of the high pressure dialogue from "Music Man". The naive reporter was absolutely stunned when he realized that what he was hearing was a complete list of wide-open answers without any legalistic double-talk. There was no mystique, just a huge dose of down-to-earth reality from a hard-working, honest guy who was determined to do the job he was hired to do. That journalist was so impressed that he came away from the interview praising the man he'd thought he was about to skewer in his next article. The article was printed soon after and was very respectful, quoting Vern often and faithfully in context. It certainly didn't paint the picture that the magazine's faithful liberals had wanted or expected, but it caused many to return to reason rather than rumor and speculation.

It was almost a year later that McPherson College's "Shop Talk" worked up the courage to beard the lion in his den. Before the interview with Vern, a budding young journalist named Cameron Randle had written the popular thoughts that "Attorney General Vern Miller is the crabgrass in the lawn of life! He's an arrogant, outspoken showman who has literally brought ruin to public office in Kansas!" "This is the attitude with which I prepared myself to confront our illustrious crusader against fun." Young Mr. Randle came away from the interview a long step closer to adulthood. To quote Randle again at a later date, he said that "I learned not only a respect for Vern Miller, but for (his) unbiased, objective thinking."

By now, the state's leading lawman wasn't just preaching to a choir consisting of policemen when he pointed at the radical increase of hard-drug usage in the state. The devastating social effects and the sky-rocketing economic damage done by the accompanying increases in the crime rate, not to mention the seldom-mentioned impact on the medical system were getting constant exposure in the press, thanks in great part to Vern. Politicians statewide jumped on the bandwagon and before long, the Law had clamped down hard on illegal drugs because every type and form of the drugs had been found in their jurisdictions ranging from marijuana, hashish, LSD, opium and heroin with all types in between. Police departments large and small across the state began launching their own anti-drug campaigns and they conducted their own raids, obviously following the example set by their energetic, enthusiastic, hard-nosed Attorney General.

Large numbers of young people, cocky and ignorant in the ways of the world and away from parental supervision for the first time make real easy marks for the cool, smooth-talking, street-wise drug dealers. The collective peer pressure seems to make something as harmless and innocuous as smoking a reefer or "toking a roach" an easy way to "fit in". As always, such social activities appear to be "cool" in the eyes of the naive youngsters because "everybody's doing it". What they don't know is exactly what's been added to spice up the effects of the rather benign appearing marijuana, such as cocaine, opium or worse and by the time they figure it out it's too late, they're hooked. The combination concoctions are much more dangerous than alcohol, which was and is usually part of the "peer atmosphere" that dealers of drugs use to set the stage for the naïve and unsuspecting youngsters.

Because of the naivete of the customer base, the university towns always have more drug traffic than non-college towns and the volume of their merchandise both attracts and generates large amounts of money. Lots of money being injected into a local economy creates a temporary surge of growth of the local businesses, so the initial euphoria of the locals distracts them from the very real damage being done while they're counting their money. Worst of all, while the attention of the adults on duty is distracted and because of the very limited experience of the younger generation combined with their cocky over-confidence, the teenagers in the area are left unguarded. That's when they're most vulnerable to the siren's song of the drug world. Vern saw it, understood it and set out to remove the drug hazard by dismantling the distribution machinery.

Before Vern was elected, it had always been a given that if a drug bust was "going down" in some of our big college towns that somehow the big dealers would not be caught with any incriminating evidence. That aroused his suspicion that someone in law enforcement was sympathetic for some reason and was warning them, but no proof of that was ever found. Then along came Vern Miller and his solution to that little problem. It was simple; he didn't tell the local police or the news media about the raids until they were already happening. He usually arranged to have both the local police and the local newsmen on the scene, too. It took a few such surprise raids to get the job done, but he'd found how to catch the sentries of the drug industry asleep. Eventually, some of the bigger dealers began getting caught with their normal inventory, which left some serious, albeit temporary holes in the drug supply chain.

Literally dozens of drug raids were planned and initiated from his office during his years in the office, netting hundreds of users, dealers, transporters and suppliers of marijuana, cocaine, heroine, hashish, LSD and many other controlled substances. It soon became apparent that some of the Prosecuting Attorneys at the city and county level had little or no experience in drug offense prosecution, so the Attorney General's office spent much of its time coaching the local Prosecutors on how to convict the suspects, while the planning process for still more raids continued. The traffickers of illegal drugs were getting a not-too-subtle message that Kansas was serious about ridding itself of their poisons.

Wichita Eagle July 30, 1974

We've all heard the old saying about how "bad pennies" keep turning up and Vern had several, but the most persistent was Don Gasser. Vern had already contributed to several of Gasser's arrests in years past, even running him down on foot and cuffing Donny himself four years earlier. Don was about to add huge credits to his resume of misdeeds.

Kansas is one of the many states that grow and process beef in large quantities and because there are always some percentage of people who covet what doesn't belong to them, we've had more than our share of different cattle/beef (meat) rustling schemes. One of the cases which received a lot of publicity involved the theft of large truckloads of stolen beef and the packing companies were taking a financial beating because of those thefts. It became so prevalent that it began to jeopardize the employment of a large number of Kansas citizens, so Vern was ready when an opportunity to break that cycle of crime presented itself. A KBI (Kansas Bureau of Investigations) officer named Carl Arbogast had received information from an informant named Kent Green who claimed that he could purchase a truck load of hanging beef from the yard of Sunflower Beef Inc, a packing house in north Wichita. Green said that he could arrange to buy one of those loaded trucks for $30,000 that night outside of Wichita. The immediate problem was to obtain that much cash and Vern quickly managed that by borrowing it from his friend Dick Saunders with the understanding that he, Vern was personally responsible for it. Then he sent word back to the informant that he (Kent Green) was to make the buy in the roadside park in Shulte, a little wide spot in the highway just outside of Wichita late that night. By the way, Kent Green was busy informing for the KBI and being as cooperative as possible in order to gain their help in reducing a completely different charge against him.

Typical of Vern, he didn't even consider delegating the assignment. He quickly called the Sedgwick County Prosecuting Attorney, Keith Sanborn to notify him of what was going to be happening in his county that night. Then he handpicked his crew from the KBI and the Sedgwick County Sheriff Deputies and set them in place after dark around the roadside park at Shulte, Kansas. Since the officers were arranged in a circle around the transfer point, he gave them strict orders not to shoot unless they were shot at first for fear of hitting one of their own men. The long and short of it is that they were not to shoot unless the bad guys fired a gun first.

The truck arrived right on schedule being followed by a car driven by Joe Teal. Some of the officers had been able to see who was behind the wheel of the car and identify him as Teal, but it was a surprise to all when Gasser climbed down from the cab of that truck. There were some formalities and as soon as Gasser had the envelope containing the money in his hand, Arbogast kicked the side of the Cadillac. Vern jumped out of the trunk and Joe Teal saw the deal going sour so he took off in the car, leaving Gasser to manage for himself. Federal ATF Agent Mike Gammage yelled to Gasser that he was under arrest, Gasser immediately jerked his arm away from Gammage's grasp and took off running through the dark with the envelope of money. He was like a halfback on the loose with a football; at first he was trying to catch the car that Teal was driving. When Gasser saw that catching a ride with Teal was futile, he turned and went right through the line of officers surrounding him and toward a railroad bed with Vern right on his heels!

Sure enough, one of the Sheriff's Jail Guards couldn't resist the temptation of a moving target. He pulled the trigger of the 12 gauge riot gun loaded with double ought buckshot like he was shooting a pheasant right out from in front of a pursuing bird dog and Vern was playing the part of the bird dog. Don knew that Vern was gaining on him when suddenly, four of the nine big pellets hit Donny, went all the way through his abdomen and he went down with Vern falling right on top of him. Gasser was hurting so much that his only choice was to be cooperative so Vern didn't bother putting cuffs on him. Don was losing blood and getting him to a hospital quickly was a necessity, so they hurriedly loaded him in the back seat of the nearest unmarked KBI sedan. Prosecuting Attorney Keith Sanborn arrived at that moment and without realizing what he was in for, he jumped in the front seat with Vern at the wheel and Gasser stretched out on the back seat. Vern was in a real hurry, sometimes hitting speeds well over 120 mph along State Highway K42 heading into Wichita to St. Francis Hospital. Keith was very tense, but very quiet each time he saw the speedometer needle get buried. Fortunately for all concerned, traffic was light on the streets that night and many of the intersections were blocked by police cars along the way. Gasser remembers watching the light poles going by at an alarming rate and he complained loudly "Dammit Vern, you'll kill us all if you don't slow down!"

The warning had gone out by radio, so a surgical team was waiting when they arrived. Within minutes, Gasser was stripped, prepped, anesthetized and the surgery proved that each of the pellets had gone all the way through Gasser's abdomen without hitting anything critical. They patched up the damaged organs, sewed him up and everybody heaved a huge sigh of relief, maybe especially Vern because he'd developed an odd fondness for the amiable criminal. I saw them; the scars are still there, testimony of a very near miss. A couple of months later Don was released from medical care and he went straight to jail. Shortly after that, another line was added to his list of convictions. Joe Teal was tried and convicted along with Gasser and both were sent to Lansing State Prison. Meantime, Sanborn allowed as how he'd definitely pass on any future invitations from Vern to go for a ride anywhere.

As with all upper management jobs, some small percentage of the work expected of the Attorney General is pure public relations work for the benefit of the State and a somewhat smaller part of that is actually enjoyable, like greeting visiting dignitaries and notables and showing them around the State Capitol. Since Vern had always been involved in motorcycling in many forms ranging from touring the highways to moto cross racing, he'd been thrilled to get to meet the greatest motorcycle stunt rider of all while he was still Sheriff and had handled the security for a motorcycle jumping exhibition by the notorious Evel Knievel. Vern got the assignment again a few years later, that time to give Knievel a guided tour of the Capitol. Here's a picture taken during the press conference, followed by another news photo of Vern in the air on his MX bike.

I wish the picture was better so you could see the grin on his face as he gets daylight under him. The Topeka Capital-Journal also ran the picture on January 9, 1972 and titled the article "Here comes Supercop."

In order to set the stage for this next story it's necessary to remind the reader(s) of the mindset of the average Kansan during the years of the Great Depression. Our economy had pretty much collapsed and was rebuilding slowly, so our gross national product (GNP) was extremely low which means that there were very few jobs in manufacturing and production. Times were very hard and the bread lines were long. It's also appropriate to quote the venerable Kansas journalist William Allen White who had written facetiously that "Once again, the (Kansas) voters staggered to the polls and voted themselves dry."

By fast forwarding ten years we'd find that this attitude had changed ever so little over those years, but the changes were certainly visible. By 1950, liquor control laws had evolved to the point that liquor could only be sold from licensed package stores while 3.2% beer could be sold from taverns and grocery stores, both during well-defined hours. The voters who were honest enough to reveal their thirst for hard liquor had voted in favor of allowing the sale of liquor by the bottle except for a few counties that chose to remain dry.

Almost grudgingly, liquor control laws were amended early in the 60's to allow private or "bottle clubs" to "hold" their customers' bottles. It was a small step, but the door was opening slowly. The way it worked was that memberships were purchased at the door, usually for $5 each, a bottle was surrendered to the barkeeper who attached the member's name to it and drinks were poured from it on request only from that member. It was a simple concept and a lot of clubs made good money from it, but it wasn't very convenient for the members. Bottles always seemed to run dry without warning right in the middle of an evening of dining and dancing, frequently causing the party-goers to make a quick trip to the nearest liquor store or a bootlegger if the stores were closed. We all knew who and where the bootleggers were and patronized them occasionally even though their prices were exorbitant.

A moment of reflection is appropriate here since we all know that no amount of legislation, regardless how perfectly written and applied will ever head off the occasional drinker who chooses to drive under the influence. Since many of those partying revelers were hurrying to the liquor stores after having had a few drinks, the best our lawman could do was to support all of the programs aimed at controlling drunk driving. In spite of our collective best efforts so far though, some folks periodically decide with their booze-fogged brains that mind-over-matter should enable them to fly without wings or that their street stock sedan is ready for the NASCAR races at Daytona. Those are nearly always the ones who are eventually involved in a fatality accident and unfortunately, someone else is frequently the fatality.

We're all aware that the laws against allowing the sale of liquor in a dry state has always tempted lots of people to pick off a little 'easy money' by sneaking liquor in to sell. It was a holdover from the days of Prohibition and the longer a state remained dry, the longer the crime continued and the bigger the profit margin while spreading the profits around to all who assisted. Bootlegging was conducted with a wink at the Law that both the buyer and seller were breaking. Most tiny towns and urban neighborhoods had at least one resident bootlegger. The bootleggers were usually just "good ol' boys" that had families and either jobs or a small business. Many of them drank some, but not much, some of them were church-going and otherwise were pretty much law-abiding citizens. Many of them were even known to be very charitable when their neighbors needed help, giving them an image similar to the fictitious Robin Hood. Dating back to the last time the British tried to drag the Colonies back into the Commonwealth, rum-running through blockades and across borders has meant that big money was involved and that same lure of high profit still exists even today in spite of the risk. During the youth of our nation, sizeable fortunes were made that have formed the foundation for many of the huge fortunes of some of the "old money" families of America today, some of which have gained national prominence that remains more than a century later. Well, Vern has always taken that "wink" at the law as an insult that he has always taken personally, so he polished his plan some more and waited.

Then one day in 1971, the Federal government formed a corporation called Amtrak after the private rail companies chose to discontinue passenger service since it was not profitable. Yes, it was a noble idea to maintain passenger transport and it was certainly well-intended, but like many great ideas it was ahead of its time and required a large amount of fine tuning to make it practical. The Feds formed Amtrak in an attempt to promote inexpensive public travel by rail and that was good. However, as with all undertakings of this magnitude a few mistakes were made along with a few oversights, one of those oversights being the sovereignty of each state that Amtrak serviced. Lacking wise guidance, the quasi-governmental Amtrak quickly assumed a 'holier than thou' attitude. Since it'd been born from and by the Federal government, Amtrak management thought that it could assume that it owned a Federal license to sell liquor by the drink on its trains in any state. They got away with it, too ...until Vern decided to test their license in court against the laws and jurisdiction of his sovereign state. In order to kick things off, he followed his usual pattern by calling the appropriate Amtrak officials who referred him to their lawyers in New York. In turn, those attorneys made it clear to Vern that their client was immune to state laws and that they were not going to stop serving liquor on their trains.

Vern decided that the proper way to proceed was to force Amtrak to defend their actions in a local court. Basically, this was the same way that the laws had been enforced against all other violators of Kansas state liquor laws, so he'd treat Amtrak like any other bootlegger. He decided that the best way would be to raid an Amtrak train, so he put KBI agents on the train in Kansas City, told them to buy liquor if possible while passing through Kansas. Sure enough, when the train arrived in Newton, it was easy to determine that they'd succeeded in buying booze enroute …and lots of it. Then he boarded the train and with a team of his officers he arrested the waiters who'd sold the liquor to the KBI agents. While Vern and his team were carrying the cases of liquor off the train, the Conductor appeared and angrily ordered the officers off of his train. He was interfering with the investigation, so he was arrested and tossed in the Harvey County Jail to cool off. The phone lines to the Amtrak home office got hot in a hurry because the train couldn't move without a Conductor and a replacement had to be flown in from Chicago so that the train could leave the following morning for California, a full day behind schedule. The type of legal action that Vern wanted had been triggered and Amtrak attorneys from New York immediately filed an injunction in Federal Court to keep Vern from raiding any more trains. Ah, that was exactly what Vern wanted. The case was quickly assigned to a special three-judge tribunal headed up by the honorable Frank Theis in a Federal court in Wichita. The request for injunction was promptly denied, opening the doors for the Attorney General to conduct more such raids if he deemed it necessary to enforce the state's laws. According to the 21st Amendment, control of liquor is the responsibility of each individual state. Small potatoes? Not at all! The Amtrak attorneys immediately appealed to the United States Supreme Court, which in turn denied "al certiorie" (refused to consider, which affirmed the ruling by the lower court). The case held precedence and immediately became the law of the land across the entire nation.

Backing up to when the news of Vern's action in Newton had broken in the news media, the airlines immediately quit serving liquor over dry states. They'd been watching the case very closely and they knew that similar cases would soon be filed against them if they didn't stop breaking the laws of Kansas and they were right. Like Vern's always said, "If you don't like a law, get it changed, but don't even think about breaking it!" Once again, he'd raised the bar and the other states quickly rose up to claim their right to control their sovereign space, destroying the myth that even a postal employee outranks a state, county or city policeman.

LEADING A LIQUOR RAID on an Amtrak train, Miller (right) hauls away booze.

Ok, back to Vern's first term in office as the Attorney General. Within the first year, Vern had made himself very unpopular with the college students by cracking down on illegal drugs, particularly marijuana since it was obviously a gateway drug. Among those younger citizens he'd been labeled as being seriously anti-fun for this, but the vast majority of the citizens who were able to vote were older, wiser and they loved him. Voter appreciation for him skyrocketed when he went public with the news that the noisy, trash-generating rock concerts were hotbeds for the sale and usage of illegal drugs and alcohol and that rock concerts were therefore, unwelcome in Kansas. As the top cop in the state, he was adamant that he wouldn't tolerate them.

A rock concert at Weir, Kansas generated evidence of drug trafficking that'd been witnessed by a sheriff from Missouri, so the Jasper County (Missouri) Prosecuting Attorney filed for an injunction against a proposed concert west of Joplin right on the Kansas-Missouri state line. Vern not only attended the circuit court hearing in Missouri, afterward he vowed to "take such action as necessary to secure the Kansas side (of the border)". One of the witnesses testifying at that hearing offered an interesting, if somewhat inflammatory opinion that Wichita was "the hashish capitol of the world" and a major distribution point in the entire country because of its geographically central location. That brought Wichita's Police Chief Merrell Kirkpatrick up snarling that it wasn't so and the discussion promptly dropped out of public view, but the subject had been brought to Vern's attention and Kirkpatrick apparently kicked his own drug task force into high gear because the traffickers immediately went deep underground.

Now I don't know if the claim that Wichita was the hash capitol of anything was true, but I know a guy who used to be in that business and he's recently told me that as soon as he saw that news article, he got out of the business that same day. He knew that even if the city cops didn't find him that Miller's Raiders would be coming through his door some night real soon.

In July of 1971, a raid in Wichita and 15 other Kansas cities resulted in the following front-page coverage.

Miller, Sheriff Johnny Darr and Wichita Police Chief Merrell Kirkpatrick were in on the raid and afterward they were ecstatic. They'd shut down the "drug stores" all over town and the message was out that this city, county and the rest of this state wasn't a good place to do drug business any more.

Not all crime is either violent or drug related. Amateur gambling of the day was a huge, leisure time business ranging from a friendly game of penny ante poker at the kitchen table, rooster fights out at Billy Bob's barn, bingo down at the neighborhood hall or church to the Vegas-style slot machines. There was big bet poker and roulette in the lodges, clubs and temples of the fraternal organizations. Horse races and sporting events are synonymous with betting and we all broke the law when we did it. We also know that at times, some or much of the gambling industry has been operated by some pretty unsavory professionals whose links to organized crime have been exposed again and again. Since there's high-profit money involved, most of our states' Attorneys General of today keep a close watch on whatever gambling is legal within their states. Vern was exceptional back then because he allowed no double standard, no favors, no exceptions, no "looking the other way" like some of his peers and predecessors. Yes, he was known far and wide on both sides of the law as a straight-shooter, a real hardass and his fame was about to spread still further.

It was common knowledge that most of the fraternal organizations and private clubs in Kansas operated illegal gaming tables and machines at some of their private gatherings and he busted them regardless of the social status of the membership. After the raids, it was something of an embarrassment for the pillars of our communities to be arrested on what they'd thought was sacred ground and off-limits for law officers. They were forced to bail themselves out of jail like common criminals, then later to stand in front of a judge to confess to having gambled illegally which cost them a small fine and operating illegal gambling machines, which cost them more than small fines. Many of Vern's friends, acquaintances and peers fell victim to his enforcement of our laws. Doctors, lawyers and corporate chiefs with lots of money and influence were caught in the net, but very few of them held a grudge. They knew that they'd broken the law and remembered that he'd warned them all repeatedly to work to change laws that they didn't agree with, but never to break them. Of course the sweet little old ladies whose favorite pastime was Wednesday night bingo down at the church would still to this day like to tar 'n feather him. He lost a lot of political support over this, but it came back before the next election. It's fun to remind him that little old ladies can be dangerous and that they hold grudges forever. He grins and shrugs that one off, too.

One of these raids in particular bears telling here because of the unusual human factors encountered during the execution of the raid. As usual in communities of this type, this incident was based on a small, local socio-political empire that'd evolved over the years in Great Bend, Kansas. Vern's office had begun receiving phone calls from some of the folks up there complaining about the unabashed gambling in and around their town, so Vern himself called their Sheriff, then the Police Chief and relayed the complaint, which of course the Sheriff and the Chief denied point blank. However, the complaints continued, so undercover agents were sent to check it out and they called back to say that the territory was wide open for gambling of all kinds. The intelligence reports indicated a serious need for attention, so a raid was quietly planned in his office.

Late one evening shortly afterward, the raiding team rendezvoused a few miles from Great Bend in the schoolyard in Ellinwood, Kansas. Assignments were handed out to more than 60 officers who'd been recruited from a dozen or more departments from around the state. There were approximately 30 police cars in the caravan, which would have drawn lots of attention out on the open highways, so they had to make their approach via the back roads and much of that without headlights. It must have been quite an unexpected spine chiller for teenaged lovers smooching furtively along those country roads to hear and see such a ghostly entourage roar past.

This particular Saturday night in Great Bend was the annual Las Vegas night at the local Petroleum Club where the socially elite were sure to congregate for a night of drinking and gambling. It was likely to be one of the biggest social events of the season, so Vern had taken special precautions to prevent a leak that a raid was coming. The raid was timed to hit all the clubs in the area simultaneously at the peak of the evening.

Late in the evening, Vern and Fred Howard, the head of the KBI called the Sheriff and Chief of Police, got them out of bed and invited them to come down to a coffee shop for a chat, which they did. The Chief and Sheriff were kept occupied long enough for the entire team to spring into action precisely at 11:45. Vern and Fred Howard then took the Chief and the Sheriff to the nearest nightclub, where the slot machines were already being loaded on the rental truck the raiding party had brought with them. The Sheriff and Police Chief played dumb, claiming surprised ignorance of such activities, so Vern and Fred took them on to the next club and several others where the same thing had already happened. Finally, the two got the drift that it was obvious that they could not possibly be unaware of what'd been going on in their jurisdiction. By this time they'd arrived at the Petroleum Club (the local country club) and found the raid in full swing. KBI Agent Ivan Peden was standing at the front door with a large handful of currency, so as the late-comers approached Vern asked cheerfully "Whatcha got there, Ivan?" The policeman replied with a grin that he'd confiscated the cash from the crap table, but nobody would claim ownership of it. Vern's not famous for having a sense of humor, but he got off a good one when he told Ivan to "Take good care of it 'cause it's going right into the school fund." He wasn't joking either.

Minutes later, the atmosphere changed radically when a somewhat inebriated City Attorney staggered into view. He was obviously very upset and angry because of the raid. When he saw Vern and the Police Chief, he ordered the Chief to arrest Vern and his men for disturbing the peace. Vern countered by saying that the City Attorney would be arrested for permitting gambling. A very tense standoff was in progress when Agent Ivan Peden tapped his General on the shoulder and cracked with a tongue-in-cheek "Don't worry, General. If we go to jail, I've got the bond money." Vern nodded, but he wasn't laughing when he turned to the Police Chief and said "Go ahead, Chief. Do your duty and arrest us". Understandably, the Chief refused the bait by holding up his hands and saying "Guys, I'm not getting involved in this."

Vern's patience was getting thinner by the second and it was obvious, so one hard look from Vern convinced even the staggering drunk that discretion is the better part of valor and that he'd better shut up. He did and somebody hustled him out of Vern's sight before the State's top cop lost his patience.

Other business called about that time as one of Vern's team leaders, a KBI officer sidled up next to Vern and said "Boss, we underestimated. We need two more trucks to haul this stuff (gambling apparatus)", so Vern authorized the renting of two additional trucks and the raid ended peacefully, leaving only the paperwork to be completed.

Topeka State Journal Oct. 4, 1971

It was a low-key, anti-climactic statement when Vern was quoted a few days later as saying that "It (Great Bend) was wide open, but it isn't now".

Lots of public posturing and legal wrangling followed, but all knew that getting caught so ridiculously red-handed made it impossible to deny or defend in the black-and-white light of a courtroom. Oddly enough, once the dust settled around the case and the legal process began to change our laws governing gambling, it became glaringly apparent that if your fraternal group or club <u>hadn't</u> been busted in Miller's raids, your club simply wasn't among the socially elite. As a matter of fact, the Elks, Moose, Masons, Knights of Columbus, Veterans of Foreign Wars, American Legion, Disabled American Veterans and many more quickly chose to make lemonade by stating publicly and proudly that they grudgingly agreed with the Attorney General's enforcement of our laws. Most of them quickly voiced their continued support for him and some even increased their support because of his proven insistence on enforcing the laws equally.

By the way, you might like to know that Vern was/is a Mason and no, the Masonic Temple did not get preferential treatment.

Miller Gets Big Haul Near Louisburg

Topeka State Journal Feb. 12, 1974

Federal undercover agents had been working for several months to locate the whereabouts of one truckload of drugs that had managed to get away from Federal agents in an earlier raid. An agent named Ray Simmons was an undercover investigator for the Attorney General and during the course of his duties he'd made contact with a man who claimed that he could supply a wholesale load of various illegal drugs if Ray could show $50,000 cash. Ray reported his findings to Vern and of course it instantly became a top priority. Opportunity was knocking and Vern answered quickly by incorporating it into his plan for a raid early the following afternoon.

As part of the deal, Ray had agreed to show $50,000 in order to gain an appointment with the sellers, so Vern and Senator Jack Steineger borrowed the cash on their signatures from the senator's bank in Kansas City. Hours later, Miller, A.G. Investigator Gary Porter and undercover agent Ray Simmons swung into action. Ray drove since he had made the contact and negotiations. Miller and Porter were in the trunk of the car armed with .30 caliber carbines. During the long trip to the meeting place, agents and Sheriff's deputies had gotten lost behind them somewhere, so they were out of sight while the deal went down. Not aware that they had no backup, Ray completed the transaction, then kicked the side of the fender. That cued Vern and Porter to pop out of the trunk with rifles held menacingly on the group of men to make it clear that trying to reach for the shotguns standing inconveniently against a tree across the driveway would be a very foolish move. It took awhile for the rest of the team to finally arrive and at the two rural residences about 20 miles south of Overland Park in a community called Louisburg, they arrested 9 people, confiscating the largest load of illegal drugs in the state's history, an estimated $328,000 worth of marijuana, cocaine and hashish.

The raid at Louisberg, as it was called in the newspapers, was the one of the high points of Vern's drug-busting career.

Wichita Eagle Dec. 18, 1974 March 7, 1975

Snitching on each other is one characteristic that most convicts have always shared, so it happened that word got to Vern that illegal drugs of all types could be obtained inside the State Prison at Lansing. The A.G.'s staff went right to work designing and setting up a means to interrupt the flow of contraband and especially drugs into the prison. Since security at the prison was very tight for all material arriving at the facility, Vern concluded that the supply line almost had to start at the County jails, especially the one in Topeka.

The Shawnee County Jail at Topeka held it's share of bad guys and it isn't surprising that they behaved pretty much like convicts in most of the other correctional institutions, including the nearby prison. One of the inmates from inside the prison got word to his contacts outside that heroin was in very short supply "inside", so a shipment was arranged. Coincidentally, Attorney General's Investigator Syd Werbin had been assigned to work under cover as a Shawnee County Jail Guard for several days and had quickly established himself as a "cooperative" guard that would look the other way for compensation during the delivery. Little did the other guards or the convicts know that Syd was the security leak that got the news to Vern that drugs were on the way and a plan to intercept the drug delivery was quickly set in motion. On the day of the delivery and to the surprise of many, the delivery guy turned out to be none other than Vern's "bad penny", Don Gasser. Don handed the heroin directly to Syd, which of course got the visiting Donny arrested on the spot. Once again, Vern became a prime contributor to Gasser's criminal rap sheet and Donny's status changed immediately from visitor to inmate. Attorneys General don't usually hang around the county jails, so when Vern walked into the room right after Donny's arrest, Gasser was surprised. Vern remembers grinning his greeting at the usually jovial Gasser and saying something to the effect that "Guy, you learn slow and then you forget."

Many years later when I interviewed Gasser, he told me that he knew the risk he'd run and that he'd been greatly disappointed when he was caught red-handed again, so he'd grinned back at Vern, shrugged and said glumly "Aw, y'win some 'n y'lose some."

**Wichita Eagle July 17, 1974 August 10, 1974 May 1, 1976
Emporia Gazetter December 26, 1974
Independence Daily Reporter December 26, 1974
Manhatten Mercury December 29, 1974**

Governor Bob Docking was serving his last term as governor because he'd announced his intention to run for a Senate seat. Then one day his recently-fired Secretary of State, Bob Brandt, walked into Vern's office one day with a story involving bribery at the highest level to obtain a large public works construction project. Vern remembers that his attention was riveted on Brandt as the story unfolded right in front of him. According to Brandt's story and the charges that resulted, the Governor's brother had arranged for a group of twelve architects to band together to submit bids on the University of Kansas Medical Center project. They would be competing for an architect's fee of $500,000. In return for a contribution of $30,000 from them which was to go to Governor Docking's 1972 campaign fund, they were told to expect to "win" the bid.

The group was constructed to appear to be a corporation with twelve equal partners, each contributing an equal percentage of their portion of the money. However, somehow the check from Sidorowicz's firm for the 'good faith' (earnest money) portion of the 'contribution' (bribe) went through architect Norbert Sidorowicz's hands to a bank where it turned into cash and from there it disappeared, never again to be tracked or recovered.

Well, Vern's concept of the Law was as it had always been, very black or white, either right or wrong according to the letter and spirit of the Law in spite of political consequences. He immediately presented the case and witness to the Judges of the Shawnee District Court, they in turn convened a Grand Jury which immediately subpoenaed the principals and their bank records. After hearing the testimony of the Grand Jury witnesses, the money trail was clear. All of the principals were indicted, but only Sidorowicz and his firm of Marshall, Brown-Sidorowicz were tried and convicted of bribery by the time Vern left office. The original indictments were almost immediately dismissed on a technicality, but new charges were filed immediately and those too were dismissed, this time by the State Supreme Court before they even went to trial. The governor's brother Dick Docking, a former governor's aide Richard Malloy and 20 others went free on a technicality. Since there was no political hay to be made by pursuing the indictments, Vern's successor as Attorney General didn't pursue the case against the rest of the men, but several political careers had been derailed and severe political damage had been done to the Democratic Party.

Within days of his initiating the case with the District Court, Vern's political support from the statewide Democratic Party had disappeared except for Sedgwick County. By living up to the letter of the law and the oath of office he'd sworn, he'd proven repeatedly that when given a choice of right or wrong, he wasn't a member of "the good ol' boys" club that would pursue their own selfish interests. They were wrong and they knew it ...and he knew it ...and the voters saw it. He was disappointed in his political peers, but not deterred. With the grace and dignity of an admirable, honorable man he responded in the manner typical of Vern Miller. Without whining or voicing bitterness at the betrayal, he and his volunteer staff maintained their positive approach, campaigned even harder and longer with the devoted, fiercely loyal voter base that he still had. When the votes were finally counted, he missed being elected Governor by less than 2,500 votes statewide. Political analysts of today are still amazed that he was able muster as many votes as he did based entirely on his name, reputation and personal popularity. It would have been a monumental success to have won while stripped of the political support of the rest of the state, an element that was and is critical for campaigning for the candidate of a major political party.

Here's the picture from Kansas City's Spice Magazine; it almost got him elected Governor of the great State of Kansas.

Governor Docking withdrew from the Senate race in the face of the scandal, Vern lost his bid for the governorship to a Republican, the office of Attorney General went to another Democrat and most of the state's elective offices reverted to Republican domination. Vern went home to Wichita knowing that he'd done the right thing, but it was not a proud time for the Democratic Party.

Leaning back in my chair and contemplating the written record of all this, I can only conclude that a very few men launched a vindictive effort to undermine a member of their own team because of greed, jealousy, spite and vengeance. You know, it's a real sad commentary on the behavior of a few people, especially when they're politicians holding elective office, that when given more power than they're morally or ethically capable of using constructively and honorably, they'll try to take the rest of their own team down with them in defeat. The irony is that it all started when they conspired to break the law for selfish gain and when they were caught trying to steal from us, they had the brass to resent being caught and prosecuted by the very system that we had elected them to operate.

Vern wearing just one of the many hats he's worn over his very active life.

Pittsburg Morning Sun, Pratt Tribune, Winfield Courier, Topeka Daily Capitol December 28, 1974
Kansas City Star, Leavenworth Times, Great Bend Tribune   December 29, 1974
Burlington Daily Republican, Lyons Daily News December 30, 1974

During the very last days of his time as Attorney General, the press discovered that the construction of a nuclear power plant was being proposed near Burlington, Kansas, which immediately brought forth the issue of nuclear waste disposal. For reasons not clear, the press sought the opinion of the Attorney General. Vern obliged with a skeptical statement in a letter drafted by his Assistant Attorney General William H. Ward that "As nuclear wastes begin to build, we find that not only is there no assurance that a way will be found to ultimately manage them successfully, but that the AEC (Atomic Energy Commission) isn't even looking very hard."   Vern added to that statement with "Consumers are blithely assured by the nuclear energy industry of the low cost of nuclear fuel. Perhaps getting nuclear fuel is cheap. Perhaps, but our customers want to know what they will have to pay to get rid of it (after the fuel has been used/depleted)."

His time in office was up, so he didn't get to pursue it, but he'd set the stage for the next administration if they wished to escalate interest. Looking back on it now, we know that both sides were right in part, but the waste site cleanups continue today...and the costs are indeed huge.

HIS FIRST PRIVATE PRACTICE

Here he was again, back in his home town of Wichita, happily hanging out his shingle and looking forward to dealing with the challenge of dealing with other people's problems while trying to help them out of their predicaments. It was a completely different approach to pretty much the same set of problems than he'd faced in his law enforcement career. The bulk of most private attorneys' cases consist of DUI's, excessive traffic tickets, assault and battery cases, civil disputes, arranging estates, marital problems and divorces, etceteras so now he was viewing those problems from a completely different perspective. Now in almost every lawyer's files there are cases that involve murder, scams 'n skulduggery, just general misbehaviors of our neighbors and I was looking for those juicy nuggets like an old hound dog constantly sniffs around searching for something to eat, but Vern just was reluctant to discuss many of his cases because of the attorney/client privilege rule. The attorney-client privilege kept the really juicy stuff under wraps. I tried halfheartedly a few times to talk him into letting me just peek a little bit into his files, but he just looked impatient and pointed me back to the piles of news articles.

He'd barely got into the swing of private practice when election time rolled around again and he saw the position he'd always wanted to try, the County Prosecuting Attorney.

While all this was going on, his private life had taken a dramatic turn for the better, too. His secretary while he'd been in Topeka followed him to Wichita and she soon became the lovely Mrs. Vern Miller. Paula had watched him throughout his terms as the Attorney General, admiring his devotion to duty and his boundless, cheerful energy, suffering with him when the trail was rough and celebrating together for the victories. Some of those years had contained some real heartbreakers, but they'd been more than offset by the astounding victories, a veritable roller coaster ride for her emotions. Nonetheless, she'd been his head cheerleader for more than four years, so marrying him was the only logical conclusion. Life was good and getting better for our guy and his family.

They bought a little acreage south of Wichita, built a modest home and raised the rest of their combined family there. They've moved into town since then, but they still own that little home in the country. It's a nice place to spend time, sort of out in the country with wildlife all around, nice neighbors and a paved road nearby that provides quick and easy access to the city.

BTK

The only reason to mention BTK here is because it's a benchmark on the timeline of Kansas history that indicates that, regardless how many good, hard-working, God-fearing people there are in any given area, there is at least one who will attempt to bring us all down. That said, let it be known that Vern had absolutely no connection to the case, not even as a consultant working quietly in the background. Vern was the Sedgwick County Prosecuting Attorney when BTK became known to the public as a serial killer. Since the police had no viable suspect to file charges against, Vern had no one to prosecute and his office was not an investigative entity unless charges had been filed, hence he had no involvement and had plenty of other cases to pursue.

SEDGWICK COUNTY PROSECUTING ATTORNEY

Vern has always been very sure of himself and his ability to get things done better than they'd ever been done by those who'd gone before him. As if to prove that he could do a better job of prosecuting for the County than the people he'd observed in that capacity, he filed for the office of Prosecuting Attorney late in 1975. He ran his usual high-energy campaign and he won easily. This was still another angle for him to observe law enforcement. Now he was able to pursue in court the conviction of people who'd been charged with crimes against society. Once again he was in a high profile, low-paying job whose greatest reward was in the accomplishment of doing it better than it'd ever been done before and, of course, he went after it with his usual enthusiastic fervor.

Wichita Eagle March 1, 1977

Running the office of Prosecuting Attorney is a real challenge and he thoroughly enjoyed that aspect of it. All that it lacked was physical exercise and he didn't get much of that on the job. But one evening Vern was among the guest speakers down at the Century II auditorium during a rally against pornography. The program was going well and he had both the honor and pleasure of sitting next to the lovely singer Anita Bryant when two streakers disrupted the speakers by racing right across the stage wearing only their big grins and tennis shoes. The pair of miscreants had obviously planned their entrance and exit by studying the layout of the stage so that they could make their escape without interference by the crowd. The first streaker succeeded in getting away to a waiting car, but Vern came off his chair like the sprinter he'd been and with a tackle reminiscent of his high school football days. He leveled the second naked streaker who was soon identified as John C. Boyd. Wichita's Chief of Police Richard LaMunyon was one of the guest speakers too and he personally arrested the naked Boyd right in front of the crowd of 2,000 cheering Christians. We sincerely hope that the disrespectful prank wasn't the sum total of John's lifetime accomplishments. He ended up being fined $250 for his foolishness.

Wichita Beacon Nov. 13, 1978

Sometime early in 1978, an entertainment promoter who introduced himself as Joey Simone arrived in Wichita and he promptly went about establishing acquaintances with the social elites. Several concerts and performances were arranged in order to further establish his legitimacy; one such event even included the venerable Bob Hope. The plot began to thicken when Simone approached a wealthy real estate broker in Wichita with a proposition that the broker front about a quarter of a million for another event which would then be funded by Adair Oil Company and then left town with it. He might've made it into obscurity with that money too if he hadn't already stolen over $200,000 from his business partner, triggering the partner to complain to Prosecuting Attorney Miller who enlisted the aid of Sheriff Johnny Darr. The two did some snooping and soon found that Simone's current girlfriend was planning a trip, so Vern and Darr followed her on a flight to New York. They'd had time to notify the New York City Police, so they were met at the plane by New York City Detectives and they all made themselves inconspicuous in the crowd until the lady hugged a man in sunglasses who'd been waiting for her. That was all they needed to recognize him and they placed him under arrest. Simone waived extradition and was immediately transported back to Wichita for prosecution. Once Simone had been fingerprinted and booked here however, it was found that he was wanted in other states by different names, so another scam artist was out of business for a few years.

$100,000 Bond Set
For Promoter Held
On Fraud Charges

By LON TETER
Staff Writer

"THIS PERSON is an escap
Miller said.

We've seen the character of our man Vern so far and here's yet another example of his commitment to his chosen profession and it provided Paula with the wildest ride of her life; the memory of it still causes her to arch her eyebrows. One Sunday in December of 1978, Prosecuting Attorney Miller and Paula were driving toward home from church in an unmarked car equipped with emergency lights, siren and police radio. Like all public prosecutors, his office had to provide one of its attorneys to be accessible to local police departments twenty-four hours of each day and this was his weekend on duty, which explains the use of a County car. They were stopped at the traffic light at MacArther and K15 when suddenly, a car literally slid to a stop beside him. As any disapproving mature adult would do, he rolled down his window and told the driver that he ought to slow down. Typical of a group of not-yet-mature adults, the boistrous young occupants flipped him off, not realizing just how unlucky they were to not only have encountered a lawman in his Sunday suit, but THE lawman! Well, as the old saying goes, if it weren't for bad luck, some folks wouldn't have any luck at all. When the traffic light turned green, the young guys did a smokey burnout as they roared away and Vern turned on the red/blue lights and siren. The chase quickly turned into a high speed pursuit well over the speed limit, endangering lives of the sparse traffic around them and Vern remembers hoping that the young driver of the car ahead of him was good enough to avoid a serious crash. Vern used the radio to call for immediate backup; he knew that there were at least several other officers in the immediate vicinity and that they would drop whatever they were doing.

The wild ride made a complete tour of the streets of Oaklawn, roaring down the quiet residential streets, through backyards and under clotheslines until the chase suddenly slid to a stop in the backyard of the house where the driver apparently lived. Vern was barely out of his car by the time he was attacked by three men plus the driver he'd been chasing. The altercation lasted for awhile and was a hair past full bloom when backup arrived. By that time Vern wasn't merely holding his own against those four guys, he was actually winning. The driver suffered some severe dental damage for sneaking up behind Vern and bonking the lawman with what was probably a flashlight, judging by the size of Vern's goose egg. Our guy had a number of lumps plus a small cut on his forehead in addition to that aforementioned goose egg, but the other guys spent time behind bars nursing their wounds for their misbehavior. None of this surprised those of us who are personally acquainted with Vern because we know that he's a trained pugilist, extremely fast and always in excellent physical condition, unlike the average tavern brawler. Aside from their bad decision to run from a cop, those guys had only managed to prove that they didn't even know how to deliver a punch once they'd managed to get within range of the elusive target that they'd so badly underestimated. The old cop was fast and he hit like the kick of a mean-tempered mule! (Remember his nickname from high school?) Members of Vern's fan club figure that the bad guys were just real lucky that police officers began arriving in large numbers because some of the rowdies would probably have suffered some real serious damage if the fight had lasted much longer.

Wichita Eagle Dec. 9, 1978

Norman Lee, also known locally as Mr. Music, was Wichita's very own big swing bandleader. His band played mostly to the over 40 crowd at the Cotillion Ballroom and the pleasant man was considered to be everybody's friend. He and his band had been well-known in the area and the Great Plains for decades, providing swing music for reunions, proms and large parties of all sorts.

Then one snowy, wintry Monday, Norman, his lovely wife Pat and their long time friend and business manager, Robert "Bo" King were found brutally murdered in the Lee's upscale home. After playing a gig at the Cotillion Club on Saturday night, Bo had loaded the band instruments and taken them to the Lee residence while the Lees had stopped for coffee with other band members. When the Lees arrived at home, they were ambushed by the killer who had already murdered Bo with a shotgun. The bodies were found by a concerned relative who had been unable to reach them by phone on Sunday and had assumed that they'd left town for the day. However, he stopped by their house early Monday evening, discovered the crime and called the Sheriff. The crime scene was now more than 24 hours old.

The media became aware of it and immediately broadcast the sad news. The brutal murders were a stunning blow to our community.

Sheriff Johnny Darr and Vern had been to a law enforcement meeting in Hutchinson the evening that the murders were discovered and were returning to Wichita when they were notified of the crime. They drove straight to the Norman Lee home on 53rd Street in north Wichita where a Deputy had found the bodies of the three victims. While they were investigating the scene, the phone rang and the caller asked to speak to District Attorney Miller. The caller was Dr. Lillia Tocker, close friend of the both the Lee and the Miller families. She asked Vern "Is it true what the radio news is saying?" When Vern answered in the affirmative, Dr. Tocker told Vern that she was sure that the killer was Charles Martin, a trumpet player in Norman's band. She had treated Martin for some time, knew that Martin was addicted to marijuana which he claimed to use to calm his nerves. However in her opinion, Charles was a mean and treacherous man who was emotionally unstable. Miller thanked her for the lead and told her that he'd check out Martin.

About that time, one of the officers came in with three empty 12 gauge shotgun shells he'd found at the scene. Because of the tremendous injuries to the victims, it was obvious that they had been killed by shotgun blasts, so now they had the beginning of a chain of traceable evidence.

While the officers were still at the scene, the phone rang again and this time it was the bus driver for the band, Jim Peterie from Hutchinson and a friend of Vern's. Peterie had also heard the news on the radio and wanted to tell Vern that he'd recently heard Charles Martin, the trumpet player, mention that if he ever decided to kill someone that he'd do it with a shotgun. Peterie also told Vern "If they were killed with a shotgun, I'll bet Martin's the killer".

On the basis of those two calls and the spent cartridges, Miller decided to check Martin out immediately. Vern, Darr and Deputy Sheriff Cliff Miller drove across town to Martin's apartment. They found it empty; all of his personal belongings had been removed and there were no clues to where he'd gone.

The next morning, Vern issued murder warrants for Martin and a nation-wide manhunt was set in motion. Over the next few weeks, Miller and Darr traveled to Arkansas, Louisiana, Oklahoma and Colorado searching through the nightclubs that had live bands for a cold blooded killer. The time dragged as they searched for Martin, but several months later, a call finally came in from a Houston Detective saying that they had Martin, but that he couldn't be questioned because he'd killed himself with a shotgun. Miller, Darr and Assistant Prosecutor Pat Connelly flew to Houston to identify Martin, but even more specifically to acquire that shotgun. Forensics tests quickly proved without a doubt that the weapon was the one that'd fired the fatal shots that had killed the Lee's and their employee.

In spite of the best efforts of all involved including his mother, Charles Martin had ended his own life leaving behind only unanswered questions and grief. His mother said later that for him, "It was the easiest way out, but it wasn't him talking when he called me. He wasn't himself. He was very mentally upset."

Wichita Eagle, March and on through the early summer of 1979

County Treasurer Walt Richardson was accused by Pamela Hicks, an employee of the Treasurer's office, of inappropriate suggestions, propositions and behavior, claiming that he had deliberately touched her inappropriately and offered her pay for days that she didn't work in return for sexual favors.

Vern was the District Attorney at the time and he arranged with the Sheriff's Department for her to wear a microphone and transmitter during a private conversation out in the country between Hicks and Richardson. That tape provided evidence of Richardson's behavior and intent. Eventually, nine other women stepped forward and all testified against him. Richardson denied any wrongdoing and even though he agreed to resign his position at one point, he changed his mind. Vern filed ouster chages and Richardson was removed from office by a three-judge panel of senior, district court judges.

Sometime during the normal stream of litigation, plea bargains and prosecutions that flow through the Prosecutor's office, a Mexican couple visiting in town found their marriage on rocky ground. The relationship reached a crisis while they were in Wichita, the husband grabbed the children and disappeared back across our southern border. The stranded wife was hysterical and called the police. Among the personal information she gave them about her husband was that he was a member of the Mexican Mafia and sure enough, the Wichita Police quickly found that the Mexican authorities were much less than cooperative.

Eventually, the case was put in the hands of the County Prosecutor's office and it was immediately assigned to Investigator Wally Hanks, Vern's first motorcycle partner who was now working for the Prosecuting Attorney. Wally soon persuaded the wife to lure her newly-estranged husband back across the border by promising him that she'd be willing to go to Mexico if he'd pick her up at the airport in Midland, Texas…and he fell for it, thinking that he had the upper hand. This incident simply reiterates one of Nature's laws that it's dangerous to get between a mother and her offspring because they won't play by any rules but their own.

Well, Wally was about to leave for Midland with her when Vern decided to go along, so off they went together. Sure enough, the errant husband showed up in the airport as agreed, swaggering arrogantly and waving a bottle of wine. The prearranged signal was that whoever the wife hugged was the husband, so when she executed her hug, Vern immediately grabbed him from behind and slammed him on the floor with the Midland Police rushing out of the crowd and piling on to get the cuffs on him. They had him for kidnapping which is a serious Federal offense. Shortly after the scuffle was over, one of the Texas policemen commented to Wally "Wow! That's your Prosecuting Attorney?! Hell, we can't even get ours out of his office!"

Not long after the arrest, the two sides negotiated trading the husband's return to Mexico for the return of the children and life returned to more or less normal for all concerned.

Wichita Eagle-Beacon Oct. 20, 1979

October of 1979 brought a great embarrassment for law enforcement in Sedgwick County; it seems that the Fraternal Order of Police decided to throw a party for its officers and for entertainment they included a nude dancer, pornographic video tapes and gambling. News of it got to Police Chief Richard LaMunyon who immediately initiated an investigation and then called to let Vern know that some of his Prosecuting Attorneys had attended. Vern called his staff together and advised them that he expected to receive their resignations immediately if they had been at that party. Seven of his attorneys and two of his investigators handed in their resignations that same day, momentarily crippling his staff. It was not a time that Kansas law officers remember with pride. However, there was an abundance of qualified attorneys and investigators available, so Vern wasted no time hiring replacements and it was only a momentary disruption for the Prosecutor's office. Training replacement police officers took much more time.

Kansas Dept of Corrections
Wichita Eagle Dec. 10, 1978 April 1980 Oct. 10, 1980

Ah, yes. I knew that sooner or later I'd have to treat the subject of Wichita's very own self-declared mafioso, George Poulos. Over his lifetime, George seems to have deliberately, almost systematically embedded himself and his criminal antics into the history of the Wichita area. For those of you who don't recognize the name, George's colorful past is a long trail of flaunting our laws and I spent many hours on the phone trying to locate him. While searching for the elusive George, I wasn't able to find anyone bearing the same last name listed in a Wichita phone book who was willing admit to me that they're related to him, but I tracked him down at one of his favorite hangouts in a smokey little pool hall on West Douglas and interviewed him briefly.

Although he seemed like a nice enough man, a very pleasant conversationalist, neatly groomed and dressed with manners to match, I knew that his felony rap sheet is a salad bar of crimes that dates back to 1948 and each of his several long prison sentences gave the law enforcement sector a welcome breather. The words bootlegger, arson, fire insurance, the fires that burned down Freddy's Brass Rail or Beachcomber Club usually pop out when his name is mentioned around the old-timers of Wichita and some of those old guys mutter that they thought that George had mob connections in Kansas City. His rap sheet includes prison-time for blowing up an airplane at Mid-Continent Airport before he got incarcerated for attempting to buy black market stolen food stamps. Several old-timers told me that George was also well-known for selling booze from the trunk of his old Cadillac in the parking lots of several nightclubs.

It's ironic that a staff reporter for the Wichita Eagle once interviewed Poulos at some length during which George claimed that he was mellowing with age, that he was "52 years old" and was quoted several times saying "I want no violence". George said a lot during the interview, mostly claiming that he was not really a bad guy. George must've really been mellow that day because he even attempted to say a few nice things about Vern including "… Vern Miller is doing his job and not bothering anybody. But if Vern gets a chance to pop you, he's going to pop you. That's the way I feel about the guy." Hmm, now that sounds like a reasonable statement from a peace-loving sort, doesn't it?

It was less than two years later when Poulos and Johnny Perez shoved a pistol in Neil Meyers' face, George took Neil's gun away from him and threatened to kill him with his with it if he didn't do business exclusively with them, referring to some stolen food stamps. Aside from attempting to traffic in stolen goods, there were a number of serious flaws in George's plan. For starters, he was threatening to kill a Wichita Police Detective who was working undercover for the Department of Agriculture, but he didn't know that. Detective Meyers was playing the part of a gangster from Kansas City and had fed George the idea that he had a truckload of stolen welfare food stamps for sale, but George didn't know that either. Meyers was a veteran officer and had already been instrumental in an investigation of the black marketing of stolen food stamps, so he knew to expect this sort of treatment. While George waved the gun around, he bragged that Wichita was his town and that only he could market all those food stamps. Also, unknown to Poulos and Perez the room was wired for sound, the entire incident was being recorded and a room full of cops were next door listening in. Yeah, I reckon ol' George had just stepped in the proverbial bucket again. When George began leaning on Neal pretty hard about where the food stamps were stashed while continuing to threaten to kill him, that's when the cops kicked the door in and flooded the room with gun-toting cops. George got his hands in the air real quick while Perez dived into the bedroom with two bullets chasing him. He came out very slowly and carefully after following the instructions to toss his gun out. Poulos and Perez were very cooperative during the process of handcuffing, then they were carted off to the jailhouse wearing their new bracelets.

The Wichita Police wasted no time filing the charges against Poulos and Perez with the Sedgwick County District Attorney, who just happened to be Vern Miller. The defense attorney was Russell Schultz, a well-known criminal-defense attorney. Vern elected to prosecute the case himself rather than assign the case to one of his assistant prosecutors and the stage was set.

It took two weeks to complete the jury selection because so many potential jurors knew George Poulos by reputation if not by personal acquaintance. Of course, both attorneys were determined to get a completely unbiased jury in order to give Poulos/Perez a fair trial. During the selection process, Vern asked one prospective juror if she knew George and she responded that she had never met him, but had heard something of his reputation. It seems that on one occasion that she had been at a Sunday school picnic and the men were attempting to start a fire to roast weiners. After suffering some frustration with the balky charcoal, several observers suggested dryly that someone should summon George Poulos to get a fire going. The lady being questioned told Vern that because of the implication, she assumed that George knew something about setting fires. Vern chuckled when he told me that "Needless to say, she was excused immediately."

The testimony of the police officers involved would've been more than sufficient to obtain an easy conviction, but Vern chose to present all evidence available, just to make sure. The fifty-three minute audiotape of the incident in the hotel room was played for the jury and George's own words and his own voice convicted him of being the ringleader during the commission of a violent felony involving a firearm. It was a slam-dunk conviction. The Judge sentenced George to fifteen years to life in the Kansas State Prison at Lansing, Perez' sentence was seven and a half to fifteen years.

A few years after George finally got out of prison he chose to run for the office of mayor of Wichita and I've been told that his primary campaign plank seemed to be to promote a gambling casino in the downtown area. Now I don't know if that's a good idea or if it was just a few years ahead of its time, but I've heard that there were some ominous mutterings among the church folks during his campaign. Well since then, Park City has obtained a dog-racing track with paramutual betting and has also declared that it wants a casino built within its boundaries. Not only that, but several other adjoining counties have shown some serious interest in the proposal, so the idea of a casino being built anywhere inside Wichita is probably moot, at least for a few years.

Kansas was, and still is, generally considered to be pretty much the heart of the Bible belt, a place where pornography is not generally acceptable. It and all that's related to it is a moral issue that has been translated into our law. At that time, it was clear that the majority of the voters wanted it outlawed and our legislators had done their best to comply with the wishes of the voters. Vern decided that the best approach would be to begin by enforcing existing obscenity law, so he staged raids at the local movie theaters that showed such films. According to the letter of the law, Vern could only seize films and books that a judge had evaluated and found that there was reasonable cause to believe that the material was obscene. He seized many offensive films and prosecuted those responsible for showing them. It wasn't long before all such theaters were closed by injunction. Miller also raided two local bookstores, Rector's and The Town Crier, confiscating books that depicted graphic sex between humans and between humans and animals. Again charges were filed and in order to get the charges dropped, the two bookstores removed the offensive material from their shelves, making it unnecessary to prosecute. Chalk up another score for the Christians.

His Second Private Practice

Vern had always wanted to practice law and one of his deputy district attorneys, Paul Clark, wanted to be the District Prosecuting Attorney, so after one four-year term in office Vern retired from public service to hang out his own shingle.

Wichita Eagle-Beacon April 18, 1981

He'd been practicing law for four months when his first murder case appeared. Louis Holloway was charged with killing Alfonso Greadington with a shotgun. During his first interview with Louis, the young man claimed convincingly that he hadn't meant to shoot and that the gun had gone off accidentally when he jacked a cartridge into the firing chamber with the trigger depressed. This caused Vern to conduct his own investigation of the operation of standard 12 gage shotguns and he confirmed what Louis had claimed.

Once in front of the jury, Vern's entire defense was that Holloway had only meant to threaten Greadington, but had been unaware that pump shotguns will discharge if the trigger is depressed when a cartridge is chambered. Vern called two policemen who'd had the same scary experience, then he called a local gunsmith to the stand who testified that nearly all pump shotguns of that vintage possess that dangerous characteristic. When Greadington had been confronted and threatened, he'd responded that he was going to put that gun where the sun don't shine. Holloway reacted with what he thought would be a threat and jacked a shell into the chamber whereupon the gun went off, killing Greadington.

The jury agreed with Vern and convicted the young man of involuntary manslaughter. Judge Robert Helsel disagreed with the verdict, although he was bound by it. The press quoted him as telling the jury that although he "Didn't understand the verdict", he said, "I will accept the verdict. I have no alternative." He went on to say "If you hear any of your friends or acquaintances talk about judges turning people loose, you tell them that it's not judges that do it, it's the juries." Young Holloway was sentenced to 1-5 years in prison for manslaughter instead of life for first-degree murder.

Vern practiced law for over 25 years, representing clients accused of everything from traffic cases upward through civil cases, divorces, adoptions, robbery, battery and even a few that had been charged with murder. From the very beginning, his philosophy was that he would not defend in court an accused that he thought was guilty, but he would represent those who admitted some degree of their guilt in order to lighten their sentence, thereby helping them to straighten out their lives. In many of those cases, negotiated sentences were arrived at in the form of plea bargains and he was very good at obtaining fair and just punishments.

It was 1985 and his law practice had just begun rolling good when his cardiologist, Dr. Tocker, pronounced him unfit to work for awhile and dragged him off to Dallas to have a mechanical coronary valve installed. Mother Nature had slowed him down once again, but he was a good patient and a good athlete, so the physical therapy was much easier for him than it would have been for most of us. So much for feeling old and tired; after that operation, the old warrior bounced back with a vengeance. He was back on his feet and back to work within a few months, but now he was much more aware of his own mortality. Sometime later, he got the latest in high-tech pacemakers, too.

Somewhere in the back of his mind was the vague realization that many of us have compiled a list of things we want or need to do before we run out of time and ability. So a year after the heart surgery Vern and his friend Leonard Sinclair rode their motorcycles up the Alaskan Highway to Anchorage and Fairbanks. They were gone for five weeks and really enjoyed it, but Vern was glad to get home and back to doing what he loved most, working at helping people get their lives back on track.

RETIREMENT

1996 came along and he'd begun to look longingly at being able to travel, to see the country that he'd defended and help to build. It'd been a long career and he needed time to relax, to reflect on his accomplishments, sorta take a breather. Besides, he wanted to find out how it felt to sleep as long as he wanted, go fishing just because the fish were there and both he and Paula wanted to travel at their leisure. He's always had motorcycles in his blood and he wanted to use the touring motorcycle he'd had for years, a pontoon boat that was perfect for fishing and lounging and a big RV with all the comforts of home, so he and Paula drove off to spend four glorious years seeing America as snowbird tourists. He made another trip up the Alaska Highway on motorcycles, this time with Larry Williams and his brother Bill who shared his love for biking. Once again, the trip was a huge success and they all came home tired and happy.

He enjoyed traveling with Paula, meeting new people every day, reveling in and admiring the society that he'd helped build on the framework of our legal system. Traveling to see the magnificent sights of our country in their motorhome was fun and interesting, touring with their friends on the motorcycle gave him still more pleasure. They even went on a Caribbean cruise, a cruise up the French Riviera, then traveled the Rhine River with former Lt. Governor Jim Francisco and his wife Julie. During this period they bought several homes and lived for a while in Apache Junction, Arizona and at Table Rock Lake in Missouri.

While Vern and Paula were living in Arizona, an unexpected phone call told them that Vern's closest and dearest old friend, Charlie Lutkie, had suffered a severe heart attack and wasn't expected to recover. Vern immediately flew back to Wichita where he found Charlie still alive, but on life-support in the Intensive Care Unit. The prognosis wasn't good, in fact it was so bad that Charlie's demise was being predicted within days at the most. Vern hung around for as long as he could endure the fidgeting until the doctor told him that he was going to remove the life-support system and that he didn't expect Charlie to survive. Vern flew back to Phoenix; he couldn't face being there when Charlie died. He'd wait for final notification that his old friend was gone. Then two days later and without warning, the phone rang and Charlie's voice said "Hey Vern! Where are ya?"

Vern was so flabbergasted that he shouted ecstatically "Charlie! Where y'calling from, Heaven or Hell?!"

Charlie responded "Well, I went to Heaven first and they wouldn't let me in, so I went on down to Hell, but they didn't want me either, so I'm back in this hospital room." They both laughed. The cheerful, barrel-chested Charlie is now 90 and can still click his heels in midair. I've seen him do it!

Vern's great love for motorcycles and cycling events has taken him pretty much around the nation including to the huge, annual Harley Davidson rally in Sturgis, South Dakota three different times. He enjoyed the massive throngs of gawkers and partying bikers being entertained by the concessionaires. It's a human circus that, like Mardi Gras, runs 24 hours a day for the duration of the huge party. By the way, the sleepy little town of Sturgis is in a beautiful setting on the rolling topography of the western Great Plains. The normal population of 7,000 souls swells to over a million every year during the three weeks of this event. Most of the tourists spend a few days to a week, living in recreational vehicles of all shapes and types ranging from sleeping bags on the ground to very expensive RV's that are equipped with everything from microwaves to satellite dishes. I've been there once and found that there wasn't nearly enough time to see all of the stage shows, displays of new and unusual bikes, trikes, competitions and social events. The big-name attraction for 2003 was G. Gordon Liddy of Watergate fame telling his story and promoting his books. The throbbing roar of multitudes of Harley engines accelerating sometimes makes it hard to sleep even far into the wee hours of the morning, so most folks are a little groggy and bleary-eyed until about mid-morning. The gallons of hot coffee, piles of good food and some leg-stretching pretty much gets everyone back to normal before noon and the carnival spools up again.

The drag races on an approved strip, the hill-climbs, the jumpers (clear air underneath them) and various other contests go on all day, some even after sundown, so throw in a little shopping among the booths, some time spent trying the multitude of different foods plus some adult stage shows and most of us are ready for some time in the ol' sleeping bag again.

The guy sporting the big grin in the photo below is unmistakably Vern. Their little motorcycle entourage had stopped to read an informational sign in the Canadian province of Alberta while enroute to Alaska.

PRIVATE PRACTICE AGAIN

As it happens to all good things, eventually the fun and novelty of retirement began to wane for him and he began to yearn again for a sense of accomplishment, of feeling as though he were contributing something. He'd been retired for four years and he'd become restless, fidgeting and looking for new things to do or see, feeling as though he was watching the rest of the world go by and he began itching to get back into it. Vern was bored stiff. Action had always been the only salve that could make that itch go away and he knew it. Explaining it to Paula wasn't easy, though. She resisted, reasoning that he'd done enough, far more than his fair share and that he should relax and enjoy what he'd earned, but that didn't ease his increasing desire to get back in the game. He rented an office from his friend and peer Danny Saville, dusted off his sheepskin and hung out his shingle again. Being a defense attorney pays lots better plus he eats, sleeps and plays on a regular schedule.

We know that each of us has potential for good and evil, some more than others and most of us strive to focus our efforts constructively. It should be clear by now that there are the few who seem to be bent on criminal intent, deliberately opposing the laws of man and some even oppose the universal laws of Nature. According to our laws, killing another human is justifiable for reasons of self-defense or to prevent the death of another, as an act of war or in defense of our country. Other than for those reasons, it's justifiable in most states only as capital punishment. This is a story of cold-blooded murder and some of the peripheral hurt that such heinous crimes cause, so if you're even slightly squeamish, you might want to skip this portion of Vern's life. Either way, just be glad that there are a few admirable men like Vern Miller around to occasionally make things right.

A MISCARRIAGE OF JUSTICE TO JOHNNY LEE WILSON

Sunday evening, April 13, 1986

In the little town of Aurora in southwest Missouri, a sweet, elderly lady named Pauline Martz was bound, robbed and brutally murdered. Her house was deliberately set on fire in an attempt to hide the crime. Johnny Lee Wilson was a mentally challenged young man who lived with his mother across town who periodically mowed Mrs. Martz's lawn, but he didn't produce a viable alibi for his whereabouts at the time of the murder. Actually, there were quite a few witnesses that could and would have provided just such an alibi if the investigating officers had thought to ask them. If the officers had investigated thoroughly, Johnny Lee would not have been charged, much less wrongly convicted.

Unfortunately for Johnny Lee, the small sheriff's department had little if any training in forensics or interrogation of criminal suspects, so Johnny Lee was easily tricked into confessing to a crime he hadn't committed and probably couldn't have committed even in defense of his own life. He was sentenced, based entirely on his own confession that had been extracted by men completely untrained to conduct such an investigation.

Not long after the discovery of the Martz murder, a man named Chris Brownfield was in the Kansas State Prison in Lansing, Kansas for a similar murder in Pittsburg, Kansas. When he heard that the retarded Johnny Lee had been convicted of Pauline Martz's murder, he became repentant. He knew that Johnny Lee was innocent of a crime that he, Brownfield and another man had committed. Brownfield called the Missouri authorities in an attempt to set it right, but the authorities didn't believe him claiming that his confession was merely a ruse to set up an escape attempt. That may have been true, but Brownfield was so frustrated with the Missouri authorities that he managed to get a call through to CBS's Connie Chung. She and her

145

team flew to Lansing and filmed an interview during which he, Brownfield confessed on film that he and a partner had robbed and murdered Pauline Martz. Brownfield withheld the trump card of the name of his partner in this crime. Then Chung and her team went to Aurora, Missouri to verify the caller's story. While interviewing Sheriff David Tatum on tape, Connie asked more pertinent questions than he seemed capable of answering. The article was aired to the public intending to arouse the ire of public attention, but only the viewing public was upset by it; nothing happened. Absolutely nothing.

The airing of the story had aroused considerable public indignation, but law enforcement officials simply didn't take any action toward solution of the problem. Because of that lack of progress, Chung's secretary Marie Patrick called Vern and described the phone call from Brownfield, the taped interview and then she asked if Vern would work on the case in an attempt to obtain justice. Vern asked why she'd called him to which she responded that Brownfield had recommended that she call Vern Miller, the former Sheriff, District Attorney and Kansas State Attorney General since he'd heard around the prison that "Vern Miller is the only one that can put that case together". Brownfield had heard about Miller from other inmates that Vern had sent to prison and even a few that he'd defended. Vern knew that it was a "pro bono" case, i.e. at his own expense, but he accepted the challenge, so Marie sent him a videotape of the "Saturday Night With Connie Chung" TV article that had already been broadcast on nation-wide television. Marie also sent a complete file of the case, including a transcript of the audiotaped confession by Johnny Lee. After viewing the tapes, he was convinced that there'd been a travesty, a gross miscarriage of justice, so he went to work.

The first thing Vern did was to drive to the Kansas State Prison at Lansing to interview convicted murderer Chris Brownsfield who was already serving a life sentence for a similar robbery-murder in Pittsburg, Kansas. After several hours of listening to Chris tell his story and asking questions, Vern concluded that the only way to put the case together was to get a statement on tape from Brownfield's alleged partner that would incriminate them in the wrongful death of Pauline Martz. Miller asked Brownfield if he would cooperate by talking on the phone to his former partner in the crime, who Brownfield now claimed had been his partner in the Martz killing and several other similar robberies. Those phone conversations would be taped and used to prove Johnny Lee Wilson's innocence. Brownfield stalled for a few days to think about it and finally agreed on condition that the calls be made from outside the prison. Brownfield also convinced Vern that his life would soon be in danger while he was there in Lansing because it would quickly become obvious to the other convicts that he was working as an informant, so Vern arranged to get him transferred to the Sedgwick County Jail. Then because of an ill-timed threat from a detective who recognized Brownfield as he was being booked in, Vern had move quickly to get Brownfield transferred to the Sumner County Jail in Wellington, Kansas where he wasn't known. Finally, he could work in relative safety. Once Chris felt safe, he called relatives, friends, ex-girlfriends and his ex-wife attempting to locate his partner-in-crime. His story to them was that he'd escaped from prison, was hiding and was broke, so he needed to collect some money that his former partner owed him. After several months, Brownfield's ex-wife came up with a phone number for the partner that she had obtained from the partner's ex-wife. She also told Brownfield that he could only be reached at 10 pm in Oklahoma City at the number she'd given him. Vern went back to the Sumner County Jail that night and the call and the contact were made. The contents of the conversation definitely incriminated the partner, so the wheels in motion to obtain a pardon for Johnny Lee Wilson.

Miller took the incriminating tape to Missouri, played the tape for Gov. Mel Carnahan's Pardon & Parole Attorney and left a copy of the tape with him to present to the Governor. Vern went home the following day to wait for results, thinking that his job was done and that he could get on with his life, but nothing happened. Vern called that attorney in Missouri so many times in the following days and months that finally he wouldn't accept any of Vern's calls while the investigation continued in the background.

The case was still getting attention from the local newspapers because politically, it was a festering sore that wouldn't heal; it was a huge political embarrassment, so finally Johnny Lee Wilson received a full pardon and apology from Governor Mel Carnahan. Once Johnny Lee was free and back at home in Aurora, the case was handed to John Frieden whose firm in Topeka had attorneys on the staff who were licensed to practice law in Missouri. Shortly afterward, they filed a civil suit against Jasper County and Sheriff David Tatum. Terms of the negotiated out-of-court settlement were quickly finalized and Johnny Lee now has a income for the rest of his life.

The name Charlie Lutkie has appeared several times throughout the story; he was Vern's Captain of the jail for as long as Vern was Sheriff of Sedgwick County. He's a spry ninety year old now. His voice is gruff, but Charlie's a friendly, congenial guy and appears as eccentric as one might expect of a man with his life experiences. He and his wife own a little tavern on South Broadway south of Haysville where truck drivers, farm hands, auto mechanics and the entire working class rub elbows with salesmen, bikers and off-duty cops. Like a neighborhood pub or cantina in almost every corner of the world, it's a great place to observe the local culture and Uncle Sam's tavern displays a fine slice of working class Americana where Vern and his friends are always welcome, although Vern rarely drinks anything stronger than soda pop. The two old policemen are still great friends. They talk on the phone several times during the week and seldom miss having lunch together once a week. Sometimes they even allow one of us youngsters to tag along.

Remember the 'bad penny'? Yes, that's Don Gasser and his name has appeared all through Vern's career. Well, nowdays Donny raises a few head of beef on his own place down in Oklahoma, but his livelihood is hauling mobil homes and big loads of hay along our busy highways. That's a real serious truckload of responsibility. He's got a lot of lives in his very capable hands every time he pulls his big rig into traffic and observers admire the skill of the guy behind the wheel of the big truck, especially when he slips on a Halloween mask to entertain children in passing cars. Yes, Donny is still mischievous.

I looked him up and spent some time talking to Donny, rode around with him in his pickup some and I couldn't help but notice that he handled that machine like a concert pianist caresses the keys of a concert grand. Naturally, I went back and reported to Vern all that I had learned about Donny, including his remarkable sense of humor. Vern listened closely, rarely interrupting even with a comment, just nodding his approval occasionally and when I was finished, he leaned back in his chair and said thoughtfully "I'm proud of him. His sense of adventure sure earned him a truckload of aggravation and very nearly got him killed more than once, but he lived long enough to grow up." There was a pause in our conversation, I waited for more and that lasted a few minutes until he finally broke the pensive silence with the revelation that "I'm glad you got to meet Donny. I like him too." The best response I could muster was a grin.

Even the gruff, irascible Charlie Lutkie likes Donny. Now just to prove that, here's just one of a seemingly endless string of mischief perpetrated by the infamous and legendary Donny Gasser. One day a few years ago, Donny had some business to take care of in his hometown of Haysville, Kansas, so when that was done he made a special trip over to Charlie's tavern and found the boss sitting on a barstool with his back to the door. Donny's never been one to pass up an opportunity for a little mischief, so he walked up behind Charlie quietly and playfully wrapped his big, long arms tightly around Charlie's shoulders while yelling "I gotcha now, Lutkie!"

There was lots of yelling, snarling and swearing and bar stools crashed on the floor. It took some doing, but Charlie finally managed to slip out of Donny's muscular grip to turn to face his assailant nose-to-nose. That's when Charlie recognized his antagonist and threatened the grinning Donny loudly with extreme bodily damage, but now it was all part of the show for the worried bystanders.

At first, the little crowd of patrons had been alarmed that an old enemy was about to wreak vengeance on their friend and they were poised to rescue him; some were grabbing chairs and beer bottles until they realized that the tall stranger had played a great prank on old Charlie. They relaxed and there was lots of hooting and hollering, back pounding and playful insults before Donny and Charlie sat down to share a pitcher of beer and play catch-up for awhile as old friends are inclined to do. Yes, the old cop Charlie Lutkie and ex-con Donny Gasser are friends.

Wichita Eagle May 14, 1994

Here's an unusual case that demonstrates once again Vern's adherence to the truth and fair play. It seems that a young man from near Wichita got himself hooked on cocaine, an easy thing to do so I'm told. Over time, he ran up quite a bill with his drug supplier who finally called in the debt. The dealer decided to apply some pressure to reclaim the debt and when it became apparent that the young man couldn't pay, the drug pusher threatened to kill his customer's parents. This threat terrified the young addict and he agonized over how to solve his problem.

Finally concluding that he had no means to satisfy his debt, he went to his parents' home and stole a .22 caliber pistol, then went to the drug supplier's house and shot him dead. He was immediately at a mortal disadvantage because the dealer's live-in girlfriend grabbed a fully automatic AK-47 and began spraying the room, trying to kill him. Fortunately for the young man, she couldn't control the weapon since full-automatic rifles buck hard and try to rise. He dove behind some furniture until she ran out of ammunition and she hurriedly attempted to reload. That's when the deadly small bore pistol came out again and several shots later she was down and dying. The young man then grabbed the AK-47 from her, finished reloading the weapon and promptly used it to shoot her and the already dead pusher in the head, then he ran. He was in custody two weeks later and remorsefully, he confessed to the murders.

Now this is where Vern got involved. The father asked Vern to represent his son, not against the murder charges because his son had confessed to them, but against what was known in Kansas as "hard 40". It's the discretionary leeway that juries of murder trials have in order to recommend a sentence that includes an additional forty years to the years assessed by the judge's guidelines. Since the addicted son had readily confessed to the two murders, it was the "hard 40" that the father feared because it would guarantee that the young man would never live long enough to make parole. It's why he begged

Vern to take the case. Of course, it was the extenuating circumstances of the threat made by the drug dealer that caused Vern to take the case.

It wasn't an easy case and there was a small album of photographs of the crime scene taken by the crime scene investigators showing the positions of the characters before, during and after the shooting stopped plus the damage to the room from the enormous number of bullets from the AK-47. Ultimately, the sentencing jury agreed with Vern; they withheld the "hard 40" recommendation. The young man will be at the very least twelve years older before he's even eligible to even be considered for parole, but he still has a chance to live a fairly normal life in freedom **IF** he behaves himself and makes a good case for his deserving parole.

As we talked about this case in his office recently, Vern was quick to point out that "I didn't lie to that jury nor was there any chicanery with my language. I didn't play any tricks with 'legalese' or fifty dollar words in order to slip one by them. I told them candidly, even bluntly that the kid was not in full control of his best judgment at the time of the crime and that he was in fear of causing his parents' deaths, so he simply made sure that he eliminated that threat to their lives." Even though it appears on the surface to be a negotiated sentence, Vern is proud of the outcome of this case because it almost surely would have resulted in a miscarriage of Justice had he failed to convince the jury.

It would be an unusual day that he didn't deal with at least several DUI's. In addition, he spends time counseling or consulting with a peer or two by phone, negotiating a marital conflict that came to blows, consulting with a client accused of car theft and maybe even dealing with some facet of a serious felony case. He's an attorney. It's what he does. Contrary to the layman's concept of what an attorney is all about, the basic philosophy of most litigators is not entirely about winning. It's about seeing that justice is dealt by our rules, our laws. Second only to assuring justice, the attorney is all about helping us get out of and through the troubles that we've gotten ourselves into.

Wichita Eagle Oct. 21, 22 & 23, 2003

Inventory counts at McConnell Air Force Base in Wichita began showing that some very interesting items were missing, such as certain items of military clothing (mostly camo fatigues) and night vision headgear. All of these items were easily saleable on the black market and a few were obtained by undercover agents, but they couldn't trace the trail back to the source until something else happened to break the case wide open. The trail to the source of the thefts of military property leads right through the heart of another, even much bigger story, so that second story must be told here first. Ok, bear in mind that there among us those who naively think that the only lessons worth learning are in a classroom, so those people don't pay attention to or believe what they see and hear in the real world. Remember the Commandment that "Thou shalt not steal"? It's in the Bible, so it's pretty basic, right? What brought these thefts and that attitude together in conflict with the Federal law was a long-standing and fully-tested law which specifically prohibits owning or even possessing fully automatic firearms, especially if it can be proven that they're stolen. The penalty for being convicted of this crime is 10 years in prison for **each** of the illegal weapons and somewhere back in history, most of these weapons had been stolen from a legitimate owner, the U.S. military.

So what would make anyone think that this Federal law didn't apply to him or that it only applied to "the other guy"? I can't imagine, but it happened recently very close to Wichita. Federal agents with a search warrant suddenly swooped down on a home in Mulvane and found sixty-six machine guns in a vault hidden behind a wall, including two of the venerable Thompson machine guns. The Thompson is a .45 caliber weapon that was used frequently by both sides of the law back during the Prohibition Era including the famous Treasury Agent Elliott Ness and it was used extensively by our GIs in combat during World War II. Gun enthusiasts know that when found, all such illegal weapons are procedurally destroyed in spite of their historical value.

Among the two hundred and sixty weapons and the sixty-six machine guns were several of the Russian-made AK-47s which are very popular among gun enthusiasts, but most are semi-automatic which makes them legal as a sport rifle. It's a well-designed and manufactured weapon of war and like all other automatic weapons such as the Thompson, it's sole reason for existing is to kill humans. These guns were not designed or manufactured to hunt animals or shoot at targets for vicarious sport; they are for killing humans, men...or women...or children. There's an abandoned AMC Gremlin in southeastern Kansas somewhere that gives silent testimony to the destructive power of this tool of war. The car is punched so full of 30 caliber holes from an AK-47 that the skeletal shell would make a better sieve than some kitchen utensils being sold off the shelves at WalMart. Well, the young man in question had invested pretty much his entire fortune in his collection, so when he bragged about it to the wrong people it wasn't long before the ATF showed up at his front door with a search warrant, two rental trucks to haul the evidence away from his home and the young man was immediately arrested.

The father of the errant young man was a local businessman, homeowner, pillar of his church and otherwise good citizen. In addition, the father had been one of Vern's good neighbors for some years, so naturally, he went to Vern to ask for help.

Vern knew the young man, so he accepted the case on one very firm condition, that his instructions be followed to the letter. He made it very clear that defending the boy wasn't going to be easy. When Vern interviewed the son shortly thereafter, he told him with dramatic emphasis that "This isn't a traffic ticket or even a DUI. You broke a very serious law and they caught you with the goods (in possession of evidence), so the only way out is to tell them everything they want to know no matter how much or who it hurts. That's the only way we can hope that the court will understand the extent your ignorance of the law and we can only hope that the court shows mercy. What they'll want are the names of everybody you've dealt with and where they can find those people, dates of all the transactions you had with them and the specific types of weapons and ammunitions involved. Don't even **think** about holding anything back because right now you're looking at over six hundred years of hard time in a Federal prison if you even stutter. You can't protect anybody and these are very serious lawmen. They don't play games with anybody and they sure won't play with you because they've got you cold." Vern also told his client "If you expect any assistance from the Federal prosecutors, you must supply the information they ask for, act as an informant and do your very best to help them make some good cases."

The young man was paying close attention and Vern had made a real believer of him. He didn't stammer or even hesitate when interviewed by the Federal law officers. The information he divulged during those interviews set several investigations in motion. His help was invaluable to the Federal officers and several good cases resulted. He was also appropriately humble in his appearance before the Federal judge during the sentencing phase.

The client did exactly as he was told and then it was Vern's turn. He began by explaining to the Federal Judge that his client had been his neighbor for a number of years; "He's a fine young man, your Honor...and has never been in trouble". Vern followed that by putting his old chief jailer, Charlie Lutkie on the stand to testify to how other inmates treat people who had worked with the lawmen and become informants. Charlie made it very clear that it's brutal. His appearance and his testimony were crucial in obtaining the lightest possible sentence and Vern took full advantage of it. When Vern asked Charlie under oath about the treatment of informants by their fellow inmates, Charlie responded in graphic terms. "They take their food away from them, they insult them, they beat them up, then they gang rape them." The defense strategy was typical Vern Miller-style "Come to God", Vern's trademark. The total cooperation with the Federal agents, total cooperation with the ATF, Charlie's testimony all combined with Vern's personal voucher got him off with five years on parole, a $7,500 cash fine plus the forfeiture of his entire gun collection. It had been an extremely expensive hobby. Had the sentencing gone any differently, that young man would have gone to prison for many years.

LUNCH WITH VERN

Life is a constant series of small adventures when you have the good fortune to spend time around a guy who's always in motion and Vern is always a hoot. More than once, just hanging around in his waiting room at lunch hour made me eligible for an invitation to lunch with, as he describes them, "some guys". He rarely defined "some guys" and I seldom thought to ask, assuming that the group would at least be civilized. Nonetheless, I armed myself with several ballpoint pens that I swiped from his desk as we hustled down the hall to a waiting car. I never had any idea what he was getting us into and he didn't bother to explain except to say cheerfully that we'd be picking up one of his sons or some guy named Paul or Richard enroute, so I just nodded, said "That's nice", then anchored myself tightly with the seat belt. Riding with him can also be an adventure of its own because he's an enthusiastic driver. Once, he almost turned the wrong way onto a one-way street in his hurry to get us to the downtown restaurant on time. Only a shouted warning from an alertpassenger averted that faux pas. He's just as enthusiastic on foot, too. I was gasping for air after the very brisk walk (I'm better at strolling than at striding) across the street and down the block.

On one of these occasions, we arrived at the elevator in the 4th National Bank Building where a small crowd was already assembled and waiting for us. I immediately recognized some of the faces and realized that I had somehow been welcomed into a gang of retired police officers and a few active judges, most of whom had either worked with or for Vern during their careers. They're a nice bunch of old guys to have lunch with, but for me it was a bit like being inserted into Robin Hood's band thirty years after the Round Table was disbanded. As I surveyed the group at the table, I noticed that there were only two guys out of maybe twenty that were younger than I and they were both judges. It was a biographer's dream and I was in heaven. Here was a large portion of Vern's inner circle, each a living legend in his own right, the handpicked core of Vern's team of warriors of years gone by and I was rubbing elbows with most of those that are still alive!

On the much smaller scale of a different day, having lunch with Vern and his closest friend Charlie Lutkie is again being invited into an inner circle. It's just as humbling too, considering some of the dangerous experiences they've shared.

It's during some of these lunches that some extremely sensitive subjects are touched on, revealing a much softer side of two men who've seen far too much and had to live with those memories after the smoke cleared and the scenes were cleaned up. Somehow, religion came into the conversation recently and the spry 90 year-old Charlie suddenly got very serious as he related a story about the Army chaplain that had helped the men in Charlie's front line combat unit during World War II. The chaplain told them that praying is as easy as a simple conversation, especially when under the severe pressure of combat. Charlie continued "Sometime later that same day, it was real dark and cold in that French forest. We were exhausted and we knew that the German troops were real close 'cause sometimes we could hear them talking. I didn't know how to pray and I 'spect I was probably real scared, so one time I wound up just making a few comments." Charlie got a faraway look in his eyes as he said reverently. "I said something like 'Lord, I could sure use a little help here'. I didn't make any wild promises or beg forgiveness for anything; I just sorta stated the fact that I needed some assistance and y'know, I guess it worked. I even felt better about all those bullets whizzing over my head." Vern nodded without adding to that. Charlie's a good example of the men that Vern had surrounded himself with throughout his entire career.

It shouldn't surprise us to find that Vern comes from a family of people who accomplish. Beginning with his father, John Miller Sr. who fought in the trenches of France and Germany during WWI. He came home, worked hard, raised a family, held a good job and built a nice home with his own hands in west Wichita. Vern's uncle Alex also fought in WWI very near where John was. By the way, Alex was the Salina attorney who encouraged Vern to attain a law degree after he'd graduated with a Bachelor's degree. The next generation of Millers produced Vern's oldest brother, John Jr. who fought in the Battle of the Bulge on the same ground that his father and uncle had fought for 30 years earlier. John Jr. came home from the war to work for the Sante Fe Railroad and during his career he rose to the position of Division Passenger Agent. After Sante Fe was taken over by Amtrak, John became the public relations officer for Amtrak in several southern states. He held that position during Vern's term as Attorney General and John even warned his superiors at Amtrak at that time that Vern wouldn't bluff or pull a punch, but they didn't listen. Vern's brother Dan was a navigator on B-24 Liberator bombing raids over Japan and retired from the Air Force as Colonel Miller; now he lives in Hawaii. Their brother George retired from the Wichita Fire Department at the rank of Battalion Chief. Vern's two sisters are also interesting characters; Wanda Farmer owns and operates Wichita's Roto Rooter franchise while half-sister Pauline Unruh was known as the dog catcher of Dodge City since she founded the Humane Society's operation there. Some years later, the cityfinally added Pauline to the payroll as the official animal control officer. Vern's daughter Jamie works for Roto Rooter, his son Cliff is a sergeant for the Sedgwick County Sheriff's Department and Marty is the Director of Botanica in the City of Wichita. Stepdaughter Lindsey and adopted son Chris finish out the immediate family and there are also eight grandchildren plus two great grandchildren. The Miller family is an impressive assemblage, both past and present. Like all the rest of us, they've had their share of headaches and heartaches, but they are admirably on the plus side for Wichita, Sedgwick County and Kansas.

Vern's story isn't over yet, but what you've seen here is as much as we've been able to assemble. By the way, I should tell you that being back in the mainstream of our legal system feels good to our guy and this is where he plans to stay for as long as he can.

Vern's resume:

High School = Wichita North, grad 1946
Military Service = U.S. Army 1946-48, served in Korea, honorable discharge
Deputy Sheriff = 1949 thru 1954
graduated from Friends University, Bachelors Bus.Adm., 1954.
Service Station owner/operator = 1954-58
Elected Sedgwick County Marshal and re-elected = 1958-62, started law school
Factory work, bill collector, service station operator = 1962-64
Elected Sedgwick County Sheriff , re-elected twice = 1964 thru 1970, graduated Oklahoma City University Law School (1966)
Elected and re-elected Kansas State Attorney General, 1970 thru 1974
Private Practice = 1975-76
Elected Sedgwick County Prosecuting Attorney = 1976 thru 1980
Private Practice = 1981-95
Retired = 1995-1999, fishing, hiking, traveling and motorcycle touring
Private Practice = 2,000-present

To list all of the sources of information and news articles that provided material for Vern's story would be an overwhelming task, but here are a few more and our sincerest thanks to all who have contributed to this recounting of Kansas history:

Textbook "John Brown to Bob Dole, Movers and Shakers In Kansas History" by Virgil Dean, University Press of Kansas
CBS Video tape of Saturday Night With Connie Chung, "Johnny Lee Wilson" aired 5/12/90
Trial transcript, State vs George Dan Poulos #80 CR 00638 dtd 10-09-80
Numerous news articles from the Wichita Eagle & Beacon, Kansas City Star, Topeka State Journal, Daily Oklahoman, Master Detective Magazine, Fort Worth Star-Telegram, Inside Detective Magazine, the Omaha World-Herald and the Hutchinson News.

ABOUT THE AUTHOR:

Mike describes himself modestly as a "…Cowboy youngster. I was born on a working ranch in the hill country of central Texas, grew up in Wichita and spent my career in the 'corporate bureaucracy', then turned to writing to amuse myself in retirement." He chuckles before adding in his best Kansas/ Texas drawl "Yeah, reckon that means that now I'm an old cowboy whut learned t'write. Gee, I wonder what I'm going to be when I grow up?"

He's been around the world, knows which fork to use at formal sit-down dinners and how to make his passport work, how to fly an airplane, how to carry on a conversation with a grizzly bear and he rarely appears in public dressed in other than bluejeans and baseball cap. In a rare serious moment he said that "Writing non-fiction is real work; writing pure fiction is fun, so I'm ready to get back to the fun stuff."